SOFT CHAOS

Bilingual Press/Editorial Bilingüe

Publisher
Gary D. Keller

Executive Editor
Karen S. Van Hooft

Associate Editors
Adriana M. Brady
Brian Ellis Cassity
Amy K. Phillips
Linda K. St. George

Address
Bilingual Press
Hispanic Research Center
Arizona State University
PO Box 875303
Tempe, AZ 85287-5303
(480) 965-3867

SOFT CHAOS

Alma Luz Villanueva

Bilingual Press/Editorial Bilingüe
Tempe, Arizona

Library of Congress Cataloging-in-Publication Data

Villanueva, Alma, 1944-
    Soft chaos / Alma Luz Villanueva.
        p. cm.
    ISBN-13: 978-1-931010-37-5
    ISBN-10: 1-931010-37-4
    I. Title.

    PS3572.I354S64 2006
    813'.54—dc22
                                                2006051376

PRINTED IN THE UNITED STATES OF AMERICA

Front cover art: Jardines del pedregal *(1994) by Alfredo Arreguín*
Cover and interior design by Aerocraft Charter Art Service

dedication

To James Marion (White Bear) Cody, my first editor and publisher,
who left the body on July 30, 2002, only to become pure spirit, play—
my friend, fellow poet, for thirty years. . . . See you later, Jim, amor siempre.

And to mi mamacita, Jesús Villanueva, whose spirit has guided me
for almost half a century in everything I've done—my poetry, fiction,
the raising of my children, her great-grandchildren. Amor siempre, Mamacita.

As a woman, I have no country.
As a woman I want no country.
As a woman, my country is the whole world.

—Virginia Woolf, *Three Guineas*

CONTENTS

SIX WHITE HORSES

six white horses

First Crow,
then Raven,
then Red-Tailed Hawk.

Crow the size of a cat—
Raven the size of a dog—
Hawk the size of a horse.

In the city of San Francisco,
my childhood city, they are
dying in great pain.

I walk the streets of my
childhood with the confidence
of a woman, with the confidence

of an Eagle, and then I see
them: Crow, Raven, Hawk:
injured, dying in great, great

pain. I want to leave this dream,
but I can't. I want to leave this
dream, but I mustn't.

Poverty, hunger, fear. Fear
of no safety. Fear
of no food. Fear

of no love. These were
my childhood teachers,
my childhood animals,

my childhood birds:
Crow, Raven, Red-Tailed Hawk.
Crow and Raven stop struggling,

but Hawk continues the battle,
the fear of no love, no love.
I kneel slowly in the dream,

I kneel and face her, Hawk,
this giant and powerful bird
who loved me, who shielded me,

as a child, Her eyes stare
into mine, fiercely fiercely.
Her love. The child.

I stand and slowly back away
from her in the dream, slowly.
Two enormous, huge, giant,

powerful White Bears stride
to each bird, tearing them,
rending them, scattering them,

eating them—I stand still,
no breath, no sound, no cry—
if they turn and see me, my

death. Then. Then White Spirit,
White Light, White Bears, each one
explodes, becoming (not the looming

terrors of my childhood, rendering
me helpless for a moment, then always
their lesson, the warrior child of heart,

of courage), they become Six White
Light Horses. Energy freed.
They rear and play, their immense

beauty in the Sun. Energy freed.
As I walk away, full of joy, the
confidence of a woman, the

confidence of an Eagle, a lovely
young man leaps to his feet
and greets me, arms around me,

tells me he loves me, how he loves
me, hands down my back, tender.
"How could I resist you?" he asks.

"I don't even know your name,"
I laugh. He smiles. "You will. I've
been waiting for you, here, forever."

I remember his name. Center of stone.
The farthest star. Sunlight on water.
Moonlight on snow. My soul spanning

centuries (life after life).
My soul always dreaming.
Freedom. Don't say it.

Don't name it. My soul
remembers the name. Of
his soul.

First dream, January 1, 1997

I am one woman

I am a seed about to burst,
I am a fern about to uncurl,
I am a bird pecking through,
I am a baby about to crown,
I am the sun about to rise,
I am a star about to shoot,
I am a woman feeling her baby turn,
I am the Earth:
                    revolving,   revolving
I am a woman giving suck,
I am a woman watching her children starve,
I am a woman who feeds stray cats,
I am a woman who couldn't care less,
I am a woman giving love for the first time,
I am a woman hoping it's over, countless times,
I am a woman about to breathe
as another begins to die,
I am a woman with a shopping list,
I am a child that runs the fastest,
I am a man that cannot cry,
I am Lorca as the bullet steals the poem,
I am a man with tender hands,
I am 6 million silent mouths,
12 million gaping eyes,
I am the child afraid to enter the oven,
I am the woman who puts her arms around him forever,
I am the woman who watches her daughter being raped,
I am the rapist that carries his darkness unconcealed,
I am one body covered in blood,
I am one body covered in kisses,
I am the galaxy:
                    revolving,   revolving
I am one woman trusting in gravity:
                    revolving,   revolving.

Spring 1977

one woman's part

The gravity of the situation, of all spinning
things (remember . . . if gravity stopped, the oceans
      would cover the land and
      oh   death   and   destruction),
is hinged on a terrific speed,   so fast
that we should be too busy throwing up
and flushing toilets to worry about
falling off (remember . . . the experiment where they
      take a bucket of water and spin
      it so fast and no water's supposed
      to spill out,   but
          it always does).
I've only recently begun to place my
trust in gravity;   I've only just begun
to accept my giddy head as part of the condition (I still do head
          stands to defy the pull, change
          the course of rivers, feel the
          body ask, what's up?)
I used to wonder why our hair didn't fly off,
      why our faces didn't fly off,
      why our skins didn't fly off,
and why a bug got to walk on the ceiling unaware
it was breaking the law
of gravity.   I've only just begun
to accept my part,
to sing my song,
to dance my dance,
to send my offering,
to join whatever it is that keeps it all
spinning.
That keeps it all spinning
for the joy of it—
that keeps it all spinning
in spite of us—
that keeps it all spinning
because it must—
because I sing, and
because I dance.
      1977

6

one woman's witness

To my daughter who learned about
gravity the same way some kids learn
about sex,
the wrong way.

I might've told you the myths of creation, created
an Earth with a boundless love,
a love so strong it glues
you to the soil: your roots
anchored with fern spore;
we scattered and sucked the round Earth.

I might've taught you songs to the seasons,
                            to the sun,
                            to the moon,
                            to the waters,
                            to the fish,
                            to the bear,
                            to the wolf,
                            to the sparrow, hawk, eagle,
                            to stone, mountain, desert, fields,
                            to the stars,
                            to the fire
in our planet, but all the songs
our people knew are echoes;
we sing without knowing tune or words,
so high and inaudible dogs whine and startle us,
                    seals surface and stare at us,
                    fish graze our skin
                                    and remember
                                    and shudder
                    the porpoise can't forget;
but what snatches I knew
I sang to you and am still learning.

I might've taught you the myths of our origins,
but they hid them from me, slyly knowing
love in its deepest form knows no

map-marked boundaries, needs no constitution
or a weekly check; consequently, I didn't
tell you lies, I just didn't know.
And so you grow up meeting others
that do not know. It was stolen from
them the second they began to breathe;
but there are those,   yes,
there are those
that sing behind silent tongues,
that spin the myths behind shining eyes,
that dare place their trust in gravity,
that gravitate toward the center
of themselves, of each other, of this planet,
to the heat,
to the core,
to the gravity that pulls
                    that dreams
                    that maddens
                    that soars
                    that sings
                    that weeps
                    that kills
                    that loves
                    that births
                    that dances,
                    and that some live/die without
knowing or believing in gravity, never knowing
they are perfectly loved: witness me
standing here.

1977

8

to Jesús Villanueva, with love

My first vivid memory of you,
Mamacita,
we made tortillas together,
yours perfect and round,
mine funny and fat—
we laughed
and named them: oso, pajarito, gatito.
My last vivid memory of you
    (except for the very last
    sacred memory
    I won't share)
Mamacita,
beautiful, thick, long, gray hair,
the eyes gone sad
with flashes of fury
when they wouldn't let you
have your chilis, your onions, your peppers
    —¿Qué saben estos gringos fregados
        acerca de *mi estómago?*—*
So when I came to comb
your beautiful, thick, long, gray hair
as we sat for hours
    (it soothed you
    my hand
    on your hair)
I brought you your chilis, your onions, your peppers.
And they'd always catch you
because you'd forget
and leave them lying open—
they'd scold you like a child
and be embarrassed like a child,
silent, repentant, angry, and secretly
waiting for my visit, the new supplies.
We laughed at our secret,
we always laughed
            you and I.

You never could understand
the rules
at clinics, welfare offices, schools,
any of it.
I did.
You lie. You push. You get.
I learned to do all this by the
third clinic day of being persistently
sent to the back of the line by 5 in the afternoon
and being so close to done by 8 in the morning.
So my lungs grew larger
and my voice got louder
and a doctor consented
to see an old lady,
and the welfare would give you the money
and the landlady would spray for cockroaches
and the store would charge the food till the check came
and the bank might cash the check if I got the nice man this time
and I'd order hot dogs and Cokes for us
at the old Crystal Palace on Market Street
and we'd sit on the steps
by the rear exit, laughing
                    you and I.

Mamacita,
I remember you proudly at Christmas
time, church at midnight services;
you wear a plain black dress,
your hair down, straight and silver,
        (you always wore it up
        tied in a kerchief,
        knotted to the side)
your face shining, your eyes clear,
your vision intact.
You play Death.
You are Death.
You quote long stanzas from a poem I've
        long forgotten:
even fitful babies hush—
such is the power of your voice,

your presence
fills us all.
The special, pregnant
silence.
Eyes and hands lifted up
imploringly and passionately,
the vision and power
offered to us.
Eyes and hands cast down
it flows through you
to us,
a gift.

You daughter, mi tía,
told me a story I'd never
heard before:
>   You were leaving Mexico
>   with your husband and two
>   older children, pregnant
>   with my mother.
>   The US customs officer
>   undid everything you so
>   preciously packed, you
>   took a sack, blew it up
>   and when he asked about
>   the contents of the sack,
>   well, you popped it with
>   your hand and shouted
>   *¡AIRE MEXICANO!*

Ayyyyyyyyy Mamacita, Jesús,
I won't forget my visions and reality
To lie, to push, to get,
just isn't
enough.

>   *"What do these damned gringos
>   know of my stomach?"
>   She refused (and pretended
>   to be unable) to speak
>   English.*

holy Ixchel,

Full of grace,
The Mystery is within you—
Blessed art thou with
All women—
And blessed is the fruit
Of our wombs, source of
All life—
Now, now, now,
And at the hour of
Our transformation into pure spirit,
Always guide us Home,
Our Goddess, Mother of
Our Universe, Ixchel.

Ixchel, give me the courage and strength
to fight back when I am
wronged—give me the courage
and strength to protect the helpless.

Give me the courage and strength
to love with a pure heart—
give me the courage and strength
to walk, day or night, without endless

fear on this Earth,
this planet of such beauty,
my Goddess, Mother of
all beings, Mother of

all time, Mother of
all space, Mother of
all healing and harm—
we are your daughters (say your names), Ixchel.

We are your sons (say your names), Ixchel.
We are your daughters, we are your sons,
heal us from harm, heal us from harm
(say your names), Ixchel.

*For the first Take Back the Night at St. Mary's College
after the rapes of young women, April 1999*

hunger

Every 3.6 seconds someone dies of
hunger on our planet—
3/4 are children under
5 years of age—
      (count 3.6 seconds . . .)
Self and other, × 4
Self and world, × 4
Dreamer, dreamt, × 4
Dancer, danced, × 4
      (count 3.6 seconds . . .)
Weeper, laugher, × 4
God, Goddess, × 4   Yes you, yes me . . .
Singer, silence, × 4
Lover, hater, × 4
      (count 3.6 seconds . . .)
Young child, old child, × 4
The Ancient Child—
Hunter, prey, × 4
Finder, seeker, × 4
      (count 3.6 seconds . . .)
Star gazer, star born, × 4
Earth bound, Galaxy bound, × 4
O passionate one,
O despairing one—
      (count 3.6 seconds . . .)
Feet on Earth, look
skyward as our planet re-
aligns with the center of our
Galaxy, great Womb of the

Milky Way—we complete
our 26,000-year cycle on
Winter Solstice, 2012, Earth
lines up to the center of the

Galaxy, to begin and
begin the next
26,000 years—O dreamer,
O dancer, hunter and prey—

The great healing light,
the great healing dark,
the great healing center of
Self and Galaxy, × 4
                    (count 3.6 seconds . . .)
May our hungers be fed,
yes you,
yes me,
self and other.
                    (count 3.6 seconds . . .)

To the Sacred Circle,
December 21, 1999

On December 21, 2012, the Solstice Sun will align with the
center of the Milky Way, an event that takes place every 26,000
years.

mystery

I am wearing my Yaqui, Spanish,
English and German skin today—
my gringa-eyes are hazel, my vision
Yaqui, my thick dark hair Spanish,

my freckles English,
my lanky structure German,
my body human, human
from this planet, Earth—

I am a spirit, a soul
in drag, at home in this
galaxy, at home on our Earth—
I put clothes on me, I decorate

this human body, a female one
that housed four human young—
I decorate with joy and pleasure, as
the galaxy is decorated with its

Mystery.

*   *   *

Why does a banana wear
yellow?
Why does an apple wear
red?
why does a cat wear
fur?
Why does a bird wear
feathers?
Why does the sky wear
stars?
Why does the moon wear
light?
Why does the sun wear
warmth?

Why does the Earth wear
oxygen?
Why do we wear human
skin?
Why is skin valued beyond the
soul?
Why is the soul so
patient?
Why is the soul so
impatient,
waiting, always waiting for
our return to the innocence of
wisdom,
when we came from the
Mystery
in the first decoration
body
temporary
home.

the dawn place

The small birds, sparrows,
come to steal bread after
bold bluejays have their
fill—rain softens

old bread, storms bring
snow to my Sierras,
my mountains where my shields
still spin, will always spin,

(this life to the next)—
I see my peak, my
mountain lake, my
dawn place where I stood

to hear the Sun booming
OMMMMMM . . . where my
wonder was reborn,
my youngest son conceived

there in my Sierras, in summer
when coyotes sing their
wild passions, calling dogs
from their safety, "Will you

run with us, will you run
with us, well-fed, fire-stroked,
human-tamed-dog . . ." and my
wolf-dog, Zeke, would join

them, once for over six weeks—
thinking he was dead, I began to
mourn him . . . one morning   wounds
and gashes, skinny to the bone,

each rib visible, fur in
horrifying clumps—he stood
in the doorway—he barely
ate, did his ritual twirls,

collapsed half-dead, with
doggy smile, father to the
wild, I see his great great
great great grandpuppies

dreaming of the well-fed,
fire-stroked, human-tamed,
human-loved ancestor, who
rides and sings in their bones

every summer, every summer,
in my Sierras as
the Sun rises *OMMMMMM*
in my dawn place.

*   *   *

I look at myself in the
morning mirror, my left
breast, the tiny scar
from a cancer scare—

the breast remains,
the scar healed—
I flex the muscles over my
breasts, they expand from

50-60 pushups in the morning,
50-60 pushups in the evening,
hand weights, leg lifts,
long walks, long swims—

gravity and I fight it out,
gravity and I dance—
"Will you run with us,
will you run with us,"

she whispers, "well-fed,
fire-stroked, human-tamed

woman . . ." I hear the Sun
behind clouds, rain, storm—

I hear the Sun *OMMMMM*
in my human heart,
in my wild heart,
in my human body,

in my wild womb
that cradles my dawn
place. I am the ancestor
who rides and sings in

your bones.
Sister of the Sun.
Daughter of the Sun.
Lover of the Sun.

Mother of the Sun
who cradles the dawn
place in her
wild wild

womb (wounded, gashed,
full, now empty) . . .
OMMMMMMMM
rising rising

always rising in the
red-streaked
womb-streaked
place of *d a w n*

> *Time of wise blood, wild wombs,*
> *empty wombs of infinite*
> *possibility—*
> *January 2000*

dawn runner

> Adolescents sense a secret, unique greatness in
> themselves that seeks expression . . . in adolescence
> the bridge is between the human mind and the
> human spirit that can transcend it.
> —Joseph Chilton Pearce, *Evolution's End*

I need to wake up in the
morning and run to the
Sun (instead I turn on
    MTV)—

I need to tell my grandparents
my dreams while they sip
1/2 coffee, 1/2 milk (instead I
    can't remember dreams)—

I need to love the softness
each day brings, the wind
at night (instead I smoke and
    drink to harden pain pain

pain)—I need to hear the Earth
sing beneath my feet, to hear
rain, clouds, sky call my
name *Beloved Child* (instead

I hear *teenager*)—
I need to run to the Sun—
Moon and Stars my ancestors—
no more wars at 17, 18, 19, 20—

do not send me to die or kill—
teach me to live—to be a hunter of
dreams and magic—teach me to be
a Dawn Runner. I will run

toward the new dawn—
I will run toward the Sun—

I will be the new human—
I will ride the Night Mare

of history to exhaustion, give
her water, feed her oats, brush
her midnight coat. Then I'll rise
at dawn to run.

To my fourth Beloved Child, Jules—
the greatness of his spirit . . .
February 2000

my next life

Spring, backyard . . . the trees,
five white-blossomed,
swaying-in-the-wind,
birds-in-the-blossoms,

trees waving goodbye
goodbye   goodbye to
me—I will not see them
next spring, sweet

guardians of my dreams,
two ancient palms framing
them . . . how many nights have
I traveled far, so far . . .

how many dawns have I
returned to your rooted
dreaming, guiding me home to
my body, to wake to wake

to your beauty . . .
the storm, gale winds,
lifted the garden glass table,
shattered—the table is

empty, clear . . .
to begin
to begin
my next life.

*   *   *

I have learned to wait
for beauty . . .
have I learned
wisdom?

I have learned to wait
for dreams . . .
have I learned
patience?

I have learned to wait
for joy . . .
have I learned
strength?

I have learned to wait
for love . . .
have I learned
nothing?

Love is in the center of
my orchids—
love is in the eyes of
my neighbor's cat—

love is in the rain merging
sand, sea—
love is in the wind that drives
me forward.

*   *   *

Nine orchids on one stem,
white white to purple,
smooth yellow labia,
hidden gifts, *count:*

1. The orchid of touch.
2. The orchid of taste.
3 The orchid of song.
4. The orchid of vision.
5. The orchid of imperfection.
6. The orchid of perfection.
7. The orchid of sorrow's joy.
8. The orchid of love's chaos.
9. The orchid of   *now*   beauty

now   human   *now*   infant   *now*
vulva   *now*   penis   *now*
eyelids   *now*   tongue   *now*
fingers   *now*   hands   *now*
feet   *now*   spine   *now*
beauty   orchid   bird   butterfly   cat   *now*

                                                    now
                              now
now

                    *   *   *

Trees: Five white-blossoming
swaying-in-the-wind
birds-in-the-blossoms
snowing . . . a small

white butterfly becomes
the white, becomes
the air, becomes
the whole, goodbye   goodbye . . .

                    *   *   *

I am the cat, the leopard,
the jaguar with the fabled
nine lives . . . I dream beneath
spring sun and moon . . .

I twitch and dream as
dolphins leap, stars find
me . . . I stand on two feet,
my seventh life calls . . .

                        March 2000

25

herding crabs

—To the women in our "genre writing circle"—
Laraine, Joanna, Kathleen, Soraya, fellow herders—
Antioch University, Los Angeles

I go searching for
peace, silence, tidal
ebb, flow, the soft
sand beach, I walk

eyes searching, ears
searching, skin
skin searching—the Sky is
more than I could've

asked for, the skin
of our Cosmos, so I
asked the Sky to show
me visions as I walked

walked, watching birds,
colors shift, clouds
merge with breath, children,
babies filled with pink

orange purple clouds, their
bellies glowing, we see
no miracle, just children,
babies breathing, our own

breath, bellies glowing—
and then, I see a woman,
tiny stick in hand, herding a
crab back to tide, life . . .

it turns away from tide,
life, to sand death dying,
she chases it poking poking poking
to the tide   the sea   to life . . .

Live, small coral-specked
crab . . . the tiny stick keeps
telling you, as the woman herds
you back to sea   to life,

I see the miracle,
I see her glowing hand,
I see the ancient clouds
rush toward me. *Live*

> *As my youngest leaves home, and I to a new life*
> *of my own in Santa Fe, New Mexico—*
> *Venice, California, July 2000*

following raindrops

(Leaving Santa Cruz, California)

Before I leave
I dip
my hands
left and right
both feet
into the chill
Pacific morning
    SEA

*   *   *

I've thrown 14 years
into a garbage bin,
saving only necessity,
essence, I've been
mothering someone for
40 years, daily
Shakti I was,
Rainbow Mother, fierce
nurturer, protector, and
muse to my children,
self other self other
    MUSE

*   *   *

(The mountains, 7,000 feet, Santa Fe, New Mexico)
And now, this other
goddess who waves
her hands (lightning),
speaks (great winds),
stomps her feet,
dances (thunder),
weeps (rain snow),
laughs (death birth
death   transformation)

*   *   *

She stamps and dances,
her belt of skulls
sways and strikes each
step, her music of
destruction   creation,
this solitary goddess,
who destroys to create,
one in her Self, maiden
mother   crone   virgin,
fierce creator, her name
    KALI

*   *   *

O KALI   O SHAKTI
O my constantly Changing
Woman—you wear
turquoise onyx   silver lightning
golden thunder   the Sun
sets in your empty womb, the
Full Moon crowns, you
give birth to forever and
ever and you also make
tamales, sweet and hot,
fresh salsa y tortillas,
you feed wild hummingbirds,
hike the mountains,
destruction and creation
in your sacred body,
in your sacred mind
soul   spirit   womb, your
skulls turn to red roses,
white roses, to thirteen
crystal skulls that
sing to me of loving
self   other   self   other
    O MY MUSE

*   *   *

(Eight days before leaving Santa Cruz)
In dreams I follow
raindrops, stare until
each one encompasses me,
then raindrop to rain-
drop I journey home . . .
Kali destroys my old
life, memory cleansed
re stored for gotten re membered
and I must die to enter the immense
RAINDROPS one by one, to
be come who I must be
this time
now
this cycle
now
maker of words, tamales,
salsa, small wonders,
the great miracles I
        WITNESS

*   *   *

I am not a wife here—
I am not a mother here—
I am not a daughter here—
I dream thirteen crystal skulls
here strung on the
waist of darkness,
darkness dances, each
skull sways and
glitters . . .

```
SKULL #1    PURA VIDA
SKULL #2    PURA NADA
SKULL #3    PURO GRITO
SKULL #4    PURO CANTO
SKULL #5    The first time
SKULL #6    The last time
SKULL #7    now   now   now
SKULL #8    WOMB JOY
SKULL #9    CUNT SORROW
SKULL #10   EVERY ORGASM
SKULL #11   BIRTHING WONDER
SKULL #12   KILLING TIME
SKULL #13   Receiving all gifts, all miracles . . .
```

   * * *

Here, I am the witness
watching Kali dance
Shakti into being,
soft-winged butterflies
rainbow butterflies,
engulf her. For me,
it is enough to follow
raindrops as I go.

And to Kali, the waitress in Needles, California,
seasoned woman, welcome omen—
August 2000

duende

Where is the duende? Through the empty arch
comes a wind, a mental wind blowing relentlessly
over the heads of the dead . . . announcing the
constant baptism of newly created things.
—Federico García Lorca, *In Search of Duende*

A slice of stone, the hues of purple
circling to delicate crystal circle in the
very center, and in the center of the
very center is space

just space
that reminds me of
why I dream
why I long to journey

to brand new places
see brand new beauty
hear brand new songs words voices
feel brand new waters earth wind light

taste brand new foods on my brand new tongue
my brand new ears brand new eyes hands feet
and my heart especially my heart is always yes
always brand new the size of that

space

*   *   *

The other day, a slice of sky in
the Sangre de Cristo mountains, I look
up to a silence of hawk wings
circling   circling

her mate comes, smaller younger
he seems, they greet the air
between them as they search
the brand new sky

food
space
food
razor sharp talons

seeking food
space food
as I do
as I do

*　　　*　　　*

A tree of light this morning after
thunder, lightning, rain and hail at
7,000 feet—in the tree of light, its
leaves fly to earth, in the tree of

light are three immense black crows,
their size defying gravity, they sit in
the tree of light as the sun shines
as the sun shines then doesn't shine

only to shine again—the three immense
black crows fly away so beautifully
without effort with joy humor even, only I
remain in the

newly pulsing
newly living
newly dying
tree of light.

child's laughter

I pay $10 to enter Taos Pueblo,
1,000-year-old earth
homes—I stand in
the center of a

circle, the spirits
pass through me clear
as wind water clouds rain—
a young man welcomes

me, a woman my age greets
me, a man selling jewelry has
my grandmother's maiden name,
LUJÁN (on a sign), yet it all feels

dead, staged, until I
come to a singing
creek . . . a young boy
(who looks like my son

at that age) smiles as his
dog rolls in the cool
water on a hot day. "He
likes the water," the boy

laughs, "I don't blame
him," I laugh back . . .
the sign says, "Don't
pet the animals" as the dog

follows me, I pet his wet nose—
I follow a dirt trail, sit by
the singing creek, a sign
says "Stay out of water" . . .

I just rest my eyes on it.
A grandfather speaks to his
horse behind me in Tiwa,
a language never to be

written or recorded, I'm
told, the language sounds
like   wind   water   clouds   rain
child's laughter . . .

As I stand to leave,
I see in bright
2 p.m. sun, bleached white
pristine men's underwear

on a hanger by
itself—I wonder if a
tourist took a photo of
real Indian underwear,

I laugh softly
and leave as I can
not bring myself to buy (or sell)
the wind I breathe (this moment).

To my ancestors, Yaqui to Pueblo—
Taos Pueblo, New Mexico
August 2000

kiva song

I walk on ancient
ground, fragile newborn
butterflies lead the
way—100 centuries

human time, joy and
sorrow lived here—
people danced, birthed,
prayed, created daily

beauty for their children—
this Pueblo knows my
heart, not my face,
this face,   yet it is

always me. The sign
says to report any
sighted snakes—I sigh.
The couple climbs down

the kiva ladder, I wait
30 seconds, they climb
back up, relieved to see
light. I climb down

balancing camera, maps,
orange juice, pack, to
the darkness, one square
patch of sunlight, enough

for me—kiva is round,
so I walk in a circle
touching the new walls
over ancient walls, spirits

peek through the new
walls, dancing, singing,

weeping, laughing (is this
    why the couple fled?) . . .

And the earth, the ancient earth
beneath my feet is fertile
with memories, rushing
to my womb, I chant as

I move in the circle,
left hand touching, "I see
your beauty, ancestors,
I feel your beauty

always, I am here, I am
here, your daughter sings
your song . . ." and more,
turning, touching, now my

right hand . . . the scent of
centuries enters me, I
want to build a fire,
feed the sacred Sipapu,

stay the night, dream
of snakes, their wisdom—
what I do is feed
the sacred

Sipapu some orange
juice, feel the fire
fill my womb, refuse
to report the snakes.

"I am here," I chant,
"I am here," I sing,
100 centuries later,
right on time,

"You know you know you
know
my heart my heart my
heart . . ."

Pecos Pueblo, New Mexico
September 2000

yellow pollen ocean seduction

> Paradise is where I am.
> —Voltaire

I walk in a sea
of yellow-blossomed
sage, late afternoon,
the yellow musky scent

of opposites, of union,
well, say it, *sex,* is
all around me, my
eyes, nose, mouth, skin

fills with this yellow
pollen ocean seduction
as I walk as I swim
in this sweet sexual

sea . . . I hear the
dry creek earth,
so soft I must be
absolutely silent . . .

"I remember water, the silk
of water over rocks, over
sage, through those trees,
my dreams journeying to the

Gulf, the sea, surging
to Turtle Beings, continents,
you with eyes the color of the
Pacific on a stormy day,

listen to my dream of
water silky water rushing rushing
through a yellow sea of
sage, listen to my

dreams, dreamer . . ."
And I do.
And I know.
Where I am.

Santa Fe, New Mexico
October 2000

KOKOPELLI

Krishna, Kokopelli, sons and lovers . . .

On the plane to San Diego, I sat
next to a young man my oldest
son's age, 38, handsome,
intelligent, I could see it at a

glance—front row, leg room,
I asked, "Is this seat taken?"
He, "It's got your name on it."
Wanting to be silent, I opened the

arts section to the famous
shot of Mrs. Robinson's lovely
upraised leg, seducing the young
Dustin Hoffman, I sigh staring out

at red-tipped wing of silver . . .
and so, we talked about his life,
my life, argued politics (he for Bush,
I for Gore)—his father in the

military, as he was, but I can see
his mother loved him well—I tell
him to read Rumi, Herman Hesse—
he tells me he secretly reads

philosophy, poetry and believes in
women's right to choose—I see
it in his eyes, the directness,
respect for women, still, I

remind myself, he travels the
world selling things (Germany,
    France, Spain, Japan) . . .
the perfect son, the perfect

lover, at any moment, place or
time, I laugh only to myself,
and let myself be charmed,
"Read Rumi," I say

as we shake hands, smiling
into each other's eyes in the
airport lobby, "I will," he
promises.

*   *   *

California, place of my birth, child
hood, adult life, my earth, I re
member a Mexican saleswoman in
Santa Cruz, as we spoke she said,

"Our people are defeated," as I
bought a rainbow, handwoven, ankle
length skirt, its label IXCHEL,
Mayan Goddess of medicine and

healing—"Our people are defeated" . . .
desk clerk at European upscale hotel,
charming French accent, passes over
me, checks in white woman first,

I have a fit . . . sweeping view of 14th floor,
complimentary bottle of wine on silver
tray, note signed by the, of course, charming
manager—in the lobby a black man

waits for service, being ignored,
I yell, "How about some service
over here," they jump, come to
serve me, "He's next," I say, "Thank

you," he sighs ("Our people are defeated")—
weird European busts line the halls,
who are these ugly white fat guys, I
wonder—before my introduction (the

visiting writer) they flambé some
thing large and dangling, I say,

"Maybe it's someone's kitty"—the
Latina students and some other rebels

giggle—I reach the podium—
I want to say, "In New Mexico I'm
recognized as myself . . . Indian, Mexican,
Mestiza, here in my sacred oh so beautiful

California my name Villanueva rings
with *illegal alien go home,* and I
tell you . . . Our people are undefeated,
that is the human race."

                 *   *   *

Three Latina students drive me to
Encinitas, 25 miles up the coast,
EconoLodge, blue lovely
Krishna is on the walls, Indian

from India family runs this
place, as I check in he's
worried about my racism, I
smile, I think, Our people are

undefeated. Blue Krishna, brown
Kokopelli, flute players and lovers
of women, the feminine—my 19-
year-old son visits for one day, I

walk the tide in the mornings, I miss
I miss la mar, our daily talks
of wave   light   song   wisdom   gifts
on the tide, I miss the surfers,

my son dancing on the water, full moon
nights when he surfed past midnight, our
morning talks—I see in him Krishna,
Kokopelli, lover of women, the feminine in

men, his mother's son—in Buddhism there's no
attachment, no man knows what it is to create
life in the body, then let it go to the world—
every*one* can know what it is to

love someone more than your own
self, much more, to willingly die,
to be that attached—
I'm attached to each of my

children, I'm attached to all my
lost loves, I'm attached to the
new ones, I'm attached to strange
babies and children, I'm attached to

the sight of parents in love with their
children, I'm attached to young lovers,
their pure spirit of play, I'm attached
to the sun   moon   stars   trees   the

ground earth I walk on, flowers
especially flowers, color of the
sky in every weather lightning thunder
rain and snow . . . when I let my

son go *good bye* to his life, me to
mine, yes it was hard, and as though
Ixchel dreamt me clearly, she
gave me SNOW when I woke up,

when I woke up from dreams and
longing in Santa Fe, falling falling silent
star snow, and I could hear Kokopelli
playing his undefeated song.

November 2000

fiercely tender

> Nobody was angry enough to speak out.
> —Mayan codex, after the Conquest

Now I understand,
now I understand—
after 40 years of mothering
since I was 15 years of age—

my last son, final and
fourth child, who I lost
in the concentration camp,
my last life, my 3-month-

old baby I left behind,
hidden, knowing he would
die—one day, in this life,
this body, this son 3 months

old, saying his name over and
over, "Jules   Jules   Jules   Jules   Jules   Jules . . ."
became "Jews   Jews   Jews   Jews   Jews . . ."
tears, gratitude, knowing we are loved,

carried beyond human understanding,
each tiny human life—
and this life, this son, third son,
as I let him go to

la vida, my final teen, wild
wild energy of endless possibility—
this time I let him go to
la vida (even as I did in the

concentration camp—there is
no death)—now, I understand,
I will not mourn his leaving,
each child's leaving, my

leaving, only to arrive—
now, I understand, each
daughter is my daughter, each
son is my son, each

mother is my mother, each
father is my father, each
lover is my lover, each
soul is my soul, there

is no death of the spirit,
the human soul, only
faces changing, only
bodies changing, only

worlds changing, only
solar suns changing, only
dreams changing, the light
we see we feel we know, into

darkness, the Void, the Womb,
sweet   fertile   wild   wild   wild
darkness   COSMOS   now
I understand, we are

the sparks of light
flying   flying   soaring
gliding   merging   searing   we are
the other's light

we are
the other's
fiery
answer

CHISPAS   SPARKS
FIRE   FIERCE
AND   ALWAYS
TENDER

Santa Fe, November 2000

47

> A person is neither a thing nor a process,
> but an opening or a clearing through which
> the Absolute can manifest.
> —Martin Heidegger

love

In the center of a rainbow,
in the center of a circle
in the sky, clouds,
light, our plane just

flew to each life's
destination—we trusted the
pilot to know the way,
the silver wings to fly us

through the rainbow,
the very center of the rainbow—
our shadow on the Earth,
winged souls, we breathe

and pray, pray
and breathe, every grown-up,
child, the baby that cries for
all of us, we breathe as

one.

*　　*　　*

I sit outside to eat
breakfast after walking in
singing tide (death life death
    life)—a homeless man stops,

"I love your hat," he says,
"Thank you," I say—he asks
where I'm from, I say, "Santa Fe
for now" . . . he's been there, also

Peru, Mexico, Chile, Guatemala
(he speaks beautiful Spanish), as
well as most of Europe it seems,
India, "The most beautiful place

I've ever been," he tells me, "and the
things that happened to me in Peru,
unbelievable, I was hexed when
I was only 19 by 3 beautiful

witches." Finally, he sits, I share
my food, order him coffee, give him
$5, tell him, "Find somewhere private,
for 3 sunrises take off your clothes,

bathe in the ocean, pray, the
Earth is the great healer."
"Sounds good to me," he says, "okay,
I'll try it." Then he goes into Larry

mode from The Three Stooges, making
me laugh, people stare at us . . . why
am I sitting with this man—
he launches into a story about

climbing the trail to Machu Picchu,
the warrior spirits he encountered,
lapsing into beautiful Spanish, and
I think, watching this alcoholic,

homeless, full of charm and
life, 50-year-old something
man, as he spins me stories,
speaks . . . I'd rather sit with

wounded, bleeding freedom
than tidy, well-dressed,
showered, moneyed, bandaged,
hidden prison pain.

*   *   *

Santa Monica, busy street,
I buy moonstone earrings, long
to buy Goddess-God in Union
statue, but I don't (they fit

in the palm of my hand),
Mom and Dad, as they make
love, Mom holding the
magic in both hands, life

death—an older woman, early
70s, stands with an empty plastic
cup, holes in her sweatshirt, her
pants, sturdy wrecked shoes, her

eyes, just waiting waiting waiting . . .
I stop as though someone has
been stabbed in front of me,
a great violence is taking place

here in beautiful Santa Monica,
light-filled, dolphin-filled ocean,
surfers dance and dance, and I
do love that joy, that ecstasy—

I stop to meet this violence,
this pain, this 70-year-old woman,
my mother, my daughter, my grandmother,
my self—I give her money, look into

her waiting eyes, she says, "No one
cares about me, thank you, bless
you, I think you've changed my
luck today," she smiles sadly,

but *she smiles*, I smile back,
"Take care of yourself, bless you,"
and I whisper, "Mamacita, mi
Mamacita," dead now for

45 years, she to whom every
poem, story, novel is written,
who taught me dreaming,
who taught me love,

who blessed me with her last human
breath, this life, this body . . .
later, as I drive, in my push-
button rented car, down

busy streets toward my life as
a writer-teacher, I see a white
haired elderly man sleeping under
dirty blankets, hard bench, I am

overwhelmed, convulsed by such
love, I think of a friend who told
me she saw, in her journey through
India, a woman sitting in the

center of a crowded street,
just sitting, radiating *love*,
mother's love, she said, and
slowly people began to sit around

the woman, my friend joined them,
she sat as close as possible, and
suddenly she began to weep openly
without shame, she felt soft

hands on her shoulders back head
and then the most exquisite, she
said, yet enduring feeling of love
that she knew had only been

waiting to be released—driving
down the busy street, overwhelmed
by this feeling, I want to park
this luxury car and sit, and see

if anyone joins me, but I know
they have places for people who
do these things in this culture, so
I continue on to my life as

writer-teacher, grateful
to have a way
to express the wisdom of
the soul. Love.

       *   *   *

This morning I swam under the
waning full moon, I swam
as Morning Star, Venus, set in
the sea of my birth, the

great Pacific, I swam
as I couldn't in my mother's
womb, I swam freely,
kicking, arms flung wide,

laughing in the cool morning
air, like a woman in love
with water and air equally,
like a woman in love with

her fellow travelers, all
of us standing like trees, flying
like birds, dancing, swimming,
dying, being

born through
the opening,
opening rainbow
circle.

Santa Monica, December 2000

sky window

Black henna tattoo on
my right hand—sun, stars,
moon in a circle, vines grow
up my fingers—white women

glare at it, African woman from
Sudan gives me half off discount
at car rental, since as a child she
wore them on hands and feet . . .

"I'm going back next year after
10 years here, my youngest graduates
college, going to live like a
queen on this retire-ment, paint

my hands and feet," she smiles.
I see the queen
in her smile—she shows
me her palms, golden spiral.

*   *   *

I go to see my mother, born
from her womb I was—
I bring her tulips, gifts, stories—
all of my stories have never made

her love me—her mother, mother of
my soul, loved me because *I was*
for her—I go walking by the bay,
great blue heron, egrets, small

perfect owl perched overhead, showing
herself to me—I walk the water's edge,
boys on bikes play as I used to at that
age, flying flying—I come

to a steel blue thing, slant
of steel curved in the center,
I lie down, perfect
sweep of sky contained by

circles, ovals, triangles—
I have journeyed to
such peace, the Universe
loves me because *I am*.

                *   *   *

I've come to see you
cannot make someone
love you,
if they can't just can't—

I try to take my womb mother to
the bay, to see the water,
the sky—instead, she
insists on watching a soap,

called "The Beach" . . . the people
in the talking box more real than
I, their stories, their pain, their joy,
more real than mine (than hers) . . .

the beach, the sky in the talking box,
more real than salt   wind   bird   sky . . .
the small perfect owl said . . .
"Grieve no

more, love my
infinite sky
window, the
golden spiral

tattooed on
each feather,
each wing,
your hand."

With gratitude for the sculpture Sky Window,
on water's edge, Berkeley Marina, for all those
who create and share beauty just because . . .
Berkeley, Califas, Winter Solstice 2000

altars

A tap on my car window,
an older Indian man asks
for the time, we begin to
talk, he's going to Taos

to a detox center, family there—
"All my art supplies were
stolen," he says, a painter—
he wears an old warm blanket

the color of the earth after rain
this snow-frozen day—
"Get in," I say, and drive him
to the Greyhound station, his ride

to Taos—he carries two small
wooden rainbow-ringed flutes,
he smells of old booze, long
graceful fingers of an artist,

he tells his story, his truth—
I listen, laugh, listen, sigh, stop
the car at the station, we hug,
"Pray for me," he says, and places

the flute on my car altar, the dash—
crystals, feathers, the prayer stick
my son made at eight, the sacred lake
that summer, now Kokopelli's flute

*   *   *

He played some notes in
the warm car, smiled and
laughed softly, walked out
to the cold snowy air,

never turned or waved,
walked slowly to the
bus station's door—I pray
for him, his healing,

and I pray
for Kokopelli,
"May he return magic,
wonder, laughter, tricks and

love to
all of us, to
all of us who
wait with altars."

Santa Fe, January 2001

infra red earth

(Dream, Santa Fe)

Parents don't watch their babies
by a cliff,
the Grand Canyon below—
how do you wake up the

sleeping ones who give
birth then forget how
to care for their young,
their own minds, their own souls—

I save one baby, the other
playfully falls—
I am not the Goddess,
but a woman trying to

see the world as whole,
beautiful in its stupidity,
stunning in its cruelty,
ravishing in its horror.

*   *   *

I will stand on the rim of
volcanoes, stare into the
matrix, first fire, first
song—I will watch

wisdom flow to the
sea—I will listen
as first words rise like
steam.

*   *   *

(Hilo, Hawaii)

A hitchhiker takes me to a
secret hot pond, known

by locals—waves enter
adding their salt, the pool,

spring-fed, surrounded by
palms—for two days storms,
rain so dense cars pull to the
side of the road—when I circle

the island, Hawaiian and white greet
me—rainforest to black sand beaches,
black lava earth mounds for
miles, wide path to sea, the pond

    new earth   new earth

As I float, sky and earth dancing, rain
splashes down up, all gone but one Hawaiian
family floating on inner tubes with their smiling
baby . . . sky   earth   hot   pond   salt   waves   dreams

    new earth   new earth

        *   *   *

(PELE)

The volcano holds the infra
red earth, I've come here
to find it, that earth,
that fire, soul

of our planet, overflowing
boundaries, our human-made
boundaries, Goddess of
fire, flow, newly made

earth, too hot, too raw
to endure, but *she endures,*
this Goddess with powerful eyes,
hands, her womb from where

all life flows, becoming rock,
sand, fertile green earth,
flowers and fruit—how can I
despair when I've seen her

new earth   new earth

flesh? I sit in front of the fireplace,
Mother Pele in stone, hands
outstretched, breasts exposed, fierce
birthing eyes, full lips, she

blesses the fire, burning
without pause for sixty-one
years   new earth   new earth
. . . the volcano, Mother Pele,

centuries, eons, time is nothing
to her—I will be fifty-seven years
old this year, my heart beating
without pause since this mother's

womb, this time, this body—
I have come to Pele . . .
Bless my heart, my womb,
both hands, my eyes, this body

new earth   new dreams

hot

My vagina is coming to life in a
new way, she pulses with a
new song—we are meant to fuck,
make love, give birth to the

new ones, but there are those
of us, yes, there are those
of us whose vaginas begin
to sing some thing mysterious,

some thing unknown,
some thing so new,
and so, I'm listening
to this new pulse

that feels like pleasure,
ecstasies I could've never
imagined. The sun rises in
my vagina.

*   *   *

Snow   snow   snow   snow
falling   falling   falling   falling
icy   air   icy   sky   icy   sun
hot   springs   hot   earth   hot   hot

I open my mouth to melting
snowflakes, up to my chin
hot   hot   springs—the night
brings   mystery   dreams   darkness,

snow glitters under great Sirius,
I glitter under great Sirius,
great Warrior, lover of cold/hot,
male/female, dark/light, silence/song,

I come to you now, my life so
lonely/full, young/old, betrayed/loved,
forgotten/remembered, I remember my
life now, what a beautiful/terrible

dream it was and how I want
to dream the rest waking/dreaming,
dreaming/waking with praise and
blame and praise for every thing.

The sun
the sun
rises in
my vagina.

Ojo Caliente, New Mexico

bright sparkling path

(Fearlessness)

As I climb the path the Ancient Ones
walked (families, elders, children,
     babies), I see god spirit mystery
Sentinel in Stone, the face exactly as

I dreamt it two years ago,
the face of fearlessness—
I've journeyed far to see this
god spirit mystery Sentinel in Stone . . .

Centuries ago you knew me, a woman
with her children, many children, a healer
with her jars of herbs, secrets, dreams,
a hunter with her snares, a grandmother

with her wisdom, singing to the wind,
water, red earth, the rainbow wings
of crows. It is me, instead of herbs
these poems I write. To sing.

                    *   *   *

I lie directly on the spring earth,
on pine needles, pine shielding me with
shade and scent, high above the valley,
songs are born here . . .

"Every life a gift
I am here   I am here
nothing wasted in the
name of love."

                    *   *   *

Dancing Goddess carved on
stone, children, birds, healing
crosses all around her, all is
dancing healing dancing healing—

the path here sparkles in the sun—
climbing ladders to the Ceremonial Cave,
kiva at the edge, place of prayer,
vision, full human joy dread sorrow to

joy, the mystery—something calls me to sit
at the edge on stone, and then I see
it, the Gate of Freedom, Sky Path,
Dreaming Stars, the Ancient Spiral . . .

drummers, singers in the pre-dawn
darkness stay awake to coax the Sun
to rise to shine once again, oh the
wonder of return.

Tsankawi, New Mexico, April 2001

plaza

I love that the town clock is
stuck at 1:45, prime time for
waking and dreaming
at 1:45 p.m. a.m.—
at 1:45 p.m. I've had breakfast,
done yoga, my 60 morning push-ups,
written at least 4-10 pages, slowly re
turned to my body, spoken to students,
the world, on Grandmother's Web, re
turned to mid-day hunger, now time to
walk, swim, type new work (or daily duties
    fully awake)—
at 1:45 a.m. I dream temples, prisons,
my grown children as newborns, toddlers,
then teens, old loves, new ones,
meeting evil, greeting death, the
lush unknown becoming visible, and

then the hours switch as I walk,
dreaming, in the plaza, rainbow
fountains leaping, palm trees
glowing with tiny lights, the
church bells toll 1:45 p.m.

as I open my eyes to stars, the wide
jungle dreaming   dancing   devouring
all illusions of time, sun and moon
marry, the clock stops forever,

only sun
only moon
only life
lived at 1:45 . . .

San José del Cabo, Baja Califas

65

(she's) gone south

South of Tropic of Cancer
south of motherhood,
south of wifehood,
south of daughterhood,
south of goodness,
south of badness,
south of loyalties, false
promises, petty betrayals,
south of marriage vows, episiotomies,
natural childbirth, saddle blocks at
15 and 17, breastfeeding and fucking too,
south of your mama and your papa, all
your cousins, any a' your relatives I ain't got
nothin' to say to (including mine, oh
yeah)—
south of martyrdom, duty to My Prescribed
Role and all that tired, worn-out
bullshit—
south of crying for what ain't my
fucking fault,
south of being responsible for the
well being and happiness of those I
cannot ever in my lifetime make
happy 'cause they so unhappy
the sunlight make them mad, fuck 'em—
south of being responsible for the
whole human race, though of course,
you know me, I'll keep trying in
my own one-person (with the help of
    Greenpeace, Amnesty Int'l, Women for Women, etc. . . . .)
dauntless way to keep trying to save the
rainforest, oceans, air, people dying
in unspeakable genocides (there but for the
    grace of Goddess go I),
children with no chance at all, such
poverty, dying of starvation every 3 or 4
seconds worldwide, so I'll continue
to bitch and moan, knowing full well

the poetry canons, Poet Laureates of
the USA ain't writin' no poetry (or prose)
like this embarrassing stuff, i.e.
human suffering,
while celebrating human joy oh joy
human kind oh human kind *human kind*—
south of age and dying, though of course
I will in my own damn way,
south of orgasms 'cause these are
new ones that I gather like pearls on
a full moon night, full round and oh
so translucent with the wisdom of my
moon,
the moon of strong longing hungry well
fed fight-for-your-life pleasure joy oh joy
kind of women who *choose to love*
'cause they feel like it—
south of men who think the
moon is barren, reflection of the
sun, only, I mean real *real*
south of any one in this frame of
mind heart soul spirit body state of
insanity,
any one who believes they don't cast
no shadows,
any one who don't just love their own
darkness,
any one who *can help not* loving their own
mystery
will despise you for loving your own
Goddess-given, hard-earned, well-deserved
LIGHT
moonlight   sunlight   starlight   soulslight
you know, the one you really truly
see by, without it
we're blind even if we
have 20/20 vision, we
ain't seeing shit—

south of standing under the full moon,
south of the Tropic of Cancer, seeing the
circle of light making love to it
no shame, oh yeah,
south of loving your bloody juicy
wise ecstasy-ridden womb, the
new one of course, made expressly for
the south south south
unknown oh so dark
mysterious   ((womb))
those civilized people run screaming
from or take it out after their
childbearing years, and
south of understanding the womb
the sweet dark basket where you
gather your self moon to moon to
sun, only gets better with age,
yes, they've been lying to you all
these years, "Take it out" they
scream "for health reasons"!!!
what they mean is "Take it out
'cause now the real get down dirty
mysterious part of your life you've
been waiting for is finally upon
you, take it out it's a sin to
feel so much" (without being tortured,
    meaning all the fucking crosses we're
supposed to gladly climb on, just lie
there while sharp nails crunch through
bones, soft flesh, crown of thorns,
please)—
south of giving up your on going un-folding
mystery, crown of roses orchids birds of paradise
lilacs night blooming jasmine honeysuckle trailing
the sweet dark basket where you
gather your self moon to moon to moon to
sun, oh yeah south oh
south *to all that,*

full-figured women with short skirts,
cropped tops showing fleshy skin

arms legs chunky glowing fluid
sen su al woman letting it all
hang out, baby on one hip, toddler
by the hand, so sure of her beauty
she stares you down, looks away
at her queenly leisure, yeah mama,
ándale . . .
skinny slinky older women in skin-tight
pants, exquisite tops, talk on cell
phones strutting their stuff, jewels on
fingers, ears, necks, glossy lips, their
eyes sharp points of light and
laughter, they pause, turn,
knowing damn well they
have the stage plain out sexy
enjoying their strut and glide and slide
and ándale oh yeah ándale . . .

south to men of soft eyes, dark
mystery of their own, many build
the pyramids now, for the tourists,
and I've swum in their pools, ordered
food and drink saying "gracias"
while looking into their eyes, some
tell me stories, secrets, their families
in Mexico City, good husbands, good
fathers—young man, scars on
his right eye, right cheekbone, light
scars like feathers, I see the
eagle dancing (poet, teacher, could-be
        friend) . . . "I wrote my father about my
life *as it is now,* I told him the truth"
his eyes dance with tears "and he told
me how proud he was to have a son like
me" . . . "All my sons are writers," I say,
we laugh, we dance, the young
eagle and I, the young eagle
who hasn't learned how to hide his
pain sorrow joy—and I see that
he hunts, not for cruelty,
to survive—we could be

friends, men like him, men of burning
lumbre chispa alma (soul), who

knows (??) in the south south,
to trust, language on a man's
tongue, I am still skeptical
after years of lies, my woman
place, my womb place, my gathering
basket will no longer gather
lies . . .

south of the Tropic of Cancer,
I enter the ocean, and as
though for the first time
my eyes
can see,
clouds of brightly-tipped-neon-yellow-heads
swim into me, I pass my hand
through them like a
dreamer in her dream,
large black fish tinged in neon
red   yellow   blue   green,
silvery snaky fish (so long)
gather at the bottom of the ocean's
sweet dark basket, her mystery
intact, yet I've seen her dream
as
her
hand
passed
through
me.

Santa María, Los Cabos,
Baja California, April 2001

soltera

I pick up the fragrant yellow-white
flower I gathered in Hawaii,
two months ago, here in Los Cabos—

I think of the Amazon women, the queen
Califa, and I see her bare-breasted,
these flowers dangling on her full

mother's breasts, crowning her long dark
hair, her wrists and ankles—perhaps this
flower or another I wouldn't know (but it's

yellow-white, fragrant), I see her strolling
the beach after swimming, seashell earrings
whispering dreams, omens, she must re-member—

her six children, newborn to teens,
home with her sisters, and as she
walks her strength is apparent, she

chooses her lovers, sometimes her own
husband the king (consort, friend, ally), and
sometimes, like today, she is Virgin, and

sometimes, like today, she is
Virgin, Morning Star melting far
horizon, Sun hissing at her neck,

lover's warmth, pale Wise Moon
singing clearly to her daughter,
"This is your fullness,

in shadow, in light,
these are your footprints
one after the other,

no one else's
no one else's,
my flower."

*   *   *

Finally, after four children (two step-heart children),
grown, two husbands, gone, various
lovers, all gone, my best friends

at such a long distance,
I study my footprints in the sand
and find them beautiful.

I take the yellow-white flower to
my swimming beach at the tip of
Baja Califas, sniff it from time to

time, then I swim with neon fish,
laughing Mexican teenagers, float in the
warmth of our sun, place the flower in

stone altar, wait for Venus
to rise, sunset skies—I buy a
silver seashell red butterfly bracelet

from a man who asks too much for it, and
if I'm soltera, alone . . . "I'm not rich," I lie (not
   about the money), my priceless footprints . . .

I hear Califa laughing as
she walks into the sea, her
footprints disappear

as my pesos disappear,
and I laugh just to
laugh (rich with

beauty).

April 2001, Los Cabos, Baja Califas

gifts

In the end these things matter most: How well did you love?
How fully did you live? How deeply did you learn to let go?
   —Buddha

Let me give you a memory of
your father, he was maybe
26—a windy, bright-sun
day in San Francisco, you about

3 years old, your brother, sister
7, 9—we bought a cheap paper kite
with tiny white stars at Mr. Wong's,
your father patiently built (on half

    his days he was capable of
great patience, self-love, the
other half self-hate)—
your brother and sister made

the tail from ripped, colorful
cloths, you helped place the glue
in key places, blowing on the glue
to dry, with your father, a game,

you almost passed out with
enthusiasm and joy—your father
and I laughed, the kite tail so
beautiful, we took it to Dolores

Park, of course your father
ran to the highest hill, carrying
you on his shoulders—then your
brother and sister ran with it, taking

turns, bringing it UP . . . your
father (the wind was strong) let
the kite fly to the end of string,
kite and beautiful tail a dancing

dot—I remember your
3-year-old face was red with
wind and pleasure, a snowflake
cap covered your ears and you

pointed up as you held the kite with
your father, feeling the wind the wind
dance through your fingers,
your brother and sister having

swinging contests below and leaping
into the wind—suddenly, your father
cut the string, it flew so fast
you never said goodbye as you sat

on your father's 26-year-old shoulders,
chubby legs dangling—later, I pointed
up to the stars, told you it had become a
star. "*Star,*" you said, with such

wisdom it broke my heart
with joy. If only your father
had known that joy, his gift
to you. Of freedom.

> *To my son Marc Jason, now older than his*
> *father (in the poem) . . . mucho amor . . .*
> *it must've been April . . .*

RELEASE

release

I travel through my
past, I fly
through my past
until I reach the

room of my regrets
where things are lost
and tattered, tinged
with sorrow, longing,

grief, such longing
to heal to heal to heal—
a man, hidden in the
corner, leaps to hold

me, he's stronger than me,
but he's cautious of
my strength—he pours
liquid over me, and I

fear he's going to burn
me, then he laughs
softly, very softly—
this oil soothes me

as the others come to greet
me, softly laughing—
I hear singing now, in
this room of release.

Dream

first corn   first butterflies

Drums, men's deep voices mingled with
boys' sweet voices, call us to
come to the plaza, I follow
the river, dust swirling my feet,

I follow voices into a small
plaza where hundreds of dancers
rest, a kiva-like building, the ladder
they enter and emerge from—the

women, girl-children, dressed in black,
sashed fertile colors tie the womb, headdress
of   butterfly   corn   rain   cloud   rainbow
soft down feathers dance in wind and sun—

the men and boy-children dressed in white,
sashed whole fox pelt swaying   dancing
becoming fox sly hunter of   stars   fertile
earth   first corn   ripe watermelon   MOON—

two large men, one wears deep red, the other
deep turquoise, ribbon shirts, raise the
prayer staff of First Corn   First Butterflies,
rainbow feathers of the south at tip, eagle feathers

north to south, dance . . . dancers lead, I follow
the dancers, the voices of the singing men and
boys, the drums, the hundred dancers
(women, men, girls, boys, two twin

    boys, four years old, double blessing,
stay close to Mom)—men on the outer
circle, inner circle women, girls,
small children in the middle,

all with pine boughs, men with rattles,
men and boys with moccasins, women
and girls barefoot (to hear the Earth more
    clearly   clearly), the many people

dance as voices rise, drums rise,
pine boughs rise fall rise fall in
rhythm, rattles spiraling speaking, one
voice, one body, one prayer, female and male

bring First Corn First Butterflies into being . . .
in the sanctuary, the altar place, only the elders
sit, men and women in shade, in reverence,
outside are two young cut pines, left and

right, beside the young pines are two
young boys, maybe ten and twelve, cradling
rifles, staring straight ahead as each dancer
honors the sanctuary with pine and rattle

as they pass, dust and sun in their
eyes, they watch unwaveringly, the sanctuary
guarded by innocence—the white priest visits
but does not enter, must not enter, cannot

enter, he smiles (these centuries later) through
clenched teeth—feast on the earth before
the sanctuary (chili with pork and chicken, fresh
   corn, mounds of sandwiches, sodas, corn chips,

juicy watermelon, small salads with beans, spicy
salsa and so much more), I sit on a bench
in the shade with Indian women as they
talk about their children, grandchildren, I'm

silent till one asks, staring into me, "Do you have
any children?" "Four grown children," I smile.
"No grandchildren yet?" a grandmother wrapped
in a butterfly shawl to her nose asks, only

glances. "I have two beautiful teenage grandchildren,"
I say, tasting clouds of earth, wind.
"Well then, let's eat," the grandmother
stands on moccasined feet, walking toward

the feast, we all follow, bend to
earth, swat flies, pile our plates,
fill our hands, arms with food, we
must be hungry from motherhood, fertility . . .

First Corn   First Butterflies . . . the grandmothers joke,
pretending to steal the other's corn or soda, the
men's voices fill the plaza, the drums, back
to the shade, we eat oh we eat the feast—

Sacred Turtle Men painted yellow, long hair
painted yellow gathered stiff at crown of
head, yellow Zia signs on their chest, whole
turtle shells dangling from their sash, turtle pieces

swaying singing turtle songs as they dance the opposite
way, twining through the dancers as they please,
inspiring challenging the hot tired dancers, frowning
smiling dancing as they please, the Sacred Turtle

Men, they take the ripest watermelons (fertile
    flesh, fertile seeds) and smash them on the
earth, women rush to gather the pieces,
pass them round—a large male dancer

rests in front of me, maybe 300 lbs.,
rolls and rolls of flesh, he sits
directly on cement porch—he turns,
"What tribe are you?" . . . he holds

a large piece of watermelon, I say,
"My people are Yaqui." "Welcome, sister,"
offering me a share, "Thank you," I take a
piece of juicy red center, quench my thirst, I want

to weep but don't, I know I don't belong
(I've been gone too long, lived my life as best
    I could, and well, yes, well), I know
I don't belong here, yet how many places

have I gone where I wasn't invited to the
feast, been acknowledged as mother, grandmother,
simply told, "Welcome, sister," offered the juicy red
center of the ripest watermelon, broken open

by Sacred Turtle Men . . .
then smiling men carrying tubs of cooked
First Corn run everywhere, I'm given
my share . . .

for the first time
in a long time
I feel
full.

(A small child sees the butterfly
tattoo on my ankle, touches it
carefully as though it might
lift and fly . . .)

> *To the San Felipe People,*
> *   to the Pueblo People, the undefeated Yaquis,*
> *   who keep the Earth alive*
> *   for all of us.*
> *First Corn Dance, May 1, 2001, New Mexico*
> *(And to the blue-eyed, dark-skinned*
> *dancer, "Welcome, brother.")*

stalker/dreamer/dancer

Woman dancer with leopard
puppet stalks the plaza,
her two legs in leopard
skin match the other two—

thin wires control head, shoulders,
legs as she stalks stalks
small children scream with
delight, adults jump till they

realize "It's only a puppet," some
nervously pet her head, give
her dollars as she stalks stalks
dogs on chains bark with

fear, they know this leopard is
real, the woman is real, the
stalker is real in the soft spring
air. This dream.

*   *   *

What do I stalk . . .
everywhere I travel on
this Earth, I've lived
(other lives, other times),

I stalk my essence,
I stalk my soul,
I stalk beauty,
I stalk wonder—

this world has sheltered
me for so long, this Earth
has loved me for so long,
my bones, my flesh, sight and song,

the thin wires of each gift,
each life, each one
real in the soft spring
air. This dream. I dance.

Santa Fe Plaza, May 2001

to Anne Frank's child

Anne, you were killed at seventeen,
everything taken from you but
your soul, your spirit, your love,
your words—

young woman of bright eyes, bright
mind and bright heart, your brief
life remains a beacon—
you died when I was barely one

year old, you could've been my
older sister, even my young young
mother, and I suppose you have been
both—I know you saw horrors,

human-made evil, I hope to never (ever)
know, yet in my soul, I know, I was
there, the young mother trying to hide
her newborn, you said, "I'll never have

a child," I say, "Your child will never
ever die." And I was right, your child
your book, keeps singing your
truth 56 years later, Anne.

May 2001

mexican dreams

Simple pleasures,
la mar, her shells,
tiny life within, under foot,
I hear them, small shell-butterflies,

side by side, breathe, dream
the journey, this continent, this
shore, this tide, I step toward
empty sand, where they

do not breathe,
do not dream
their journey home,
night stars, side by

side, I wish to live gathering
empty seashells, empty hours,
empty days, empty years,
full of mysterious, simple
pleasures.

*   *   *

Early June, fifteen wetbacks died
in the borderlands, USA/MEXICO,
parched tongues, parched skin, backs, eyes,
dreams, trying to cross into USA, the border

my grandparents crossed 84 years ago,
my grandmother's people, the Yaqui,
residents of this continent, this land
for centuries, the trade routes

closed, the human journey,
urge to follow north to
east to west to south,
urge to follow dreams,

the trade routes closed.
In April I journeyed south, Baja,
snorkeled, wandered, sat under stars,
fresh tamales in plaza, rainbow fountains,

singing teen juggling fire, children playing,
families watching, peaceful scented air,
Spanish, Indian in my ears, my childhood
tongues welcome me gently gently, sometimes

not so gently, Baja drivers have no fear of death,
La Virgen guards the roads, altars stuffed
with flowers, candles, offerings, I add mine as
I go. Bells wake me at 3 a.m. louder louder, a pure

white cow leads 6 or 7 black cows, each one bell
ringing, down the dirt road where cars zip by all
day—the cows are free in Mexico to follow their
dreams of new grass, sweet water, pre-dawn air,

becoming wild cows
wild hooves, wild earth,
they thunder past, I close
my eyes to wild Mexican

dreams.

*   *   *

I am the cow that jumped over the
Milky Way, I am the cow that jumped
over the Universe, I am the cow that
jumped over the USA-MEXICO border,

I am the cow of freedom, wild nights
and wild stars, follow me . . . I am the
cow that brings water and dreams to
parched tongues, skin, eyes, my wetback

people, my glistening, shining, dreaming
wetback people, I am the cow that fed you as a
child, from my Milky Way body, my body knows
no borders, only hunger to be fed, I am

The Virgin, Isis, Shing Moo, Tara,
Changing Woman, Ixchel, Quan Yin, Great
Mother, Great Warrior, my milk has fed all
life . . . I open my eyes, my eyes . . .

the air belongs to
no one . . . I breathe
the sky with billions, gift of
trees, green plants, wetback workers

who sing in the pre-dawn fields in USA,
hunched over weeding, picking simple pleasures
for our tables, dying to get here they give us their
daily life so cheap, yet they sing with joy, great

simple pleasure. They know
the air belongs to no one,
not joy, and not their
Mexican dreams.

To the fifteen human beings who died crossing, June 2001

open lens

Early morning Venice Beach, four
teen Mexican women surround some
thing, looking down at the sand,
sad, sober, silent—

joining them, I see it—
altar of single sunflower, wild
flowers, long green reeds, slightly
swaying in morning air, red votive

candle burned into dawn, spirals
of shells holding prayers, wishes,
lost and found, lost and found—
in the sand, buried photo of

man, woman, four children from
maybe 7 to 14, all smiling into
open lens—I show the photo to
the teens, "Wonder what happened?"

one asks—I place the photo firmly in the
sand under sunflower and wonder which
family member mourns the others, their
tribe—I see my 4 children, ages 20 to

41, all gone to la vida, I'm no one's
wife—every night before I dream,
I light my memory candle, my spiral
stars, my endless wildflowers, my virgin

shore swept new each dawn, and as
I dream each one begins una chispa,
a spark, in my empty womb, my body
re-members mourning joy such joy—

in dreams, at dawn, I am mother
and child, mourner and lover, creator
of my tribe, virgin at the gate of Wonder.
I pass through. The

open lens.

Venice Beach, Califas, June 2001

furious heart

So, this is what happens to
volcanoes in a million years or so,
this—they become sky
catchers, cloud catchers, star,

sun and moon, soul and spirit
catchers, and, yes, dream catchers,
they catch our dreams day and night,
the waking dream—every living thing

dreams, these mountains re-member dreams
of hummingbird to human, each furious heart
that fights for its sip of nectar, and so generously
shares the taste *in words,* in song,

in flight. Flesh and blood,
wing and feather, brief spark/chispa in magma
flow—the soul/spirit, the volcanoes, the Dream,
our creation. In time.

> *To Rudolfo Anaya—From our conversation,*
> *your porch facing the sky catchers, their dancing*
> *spirits, never-ending joy . . . (Siempre, gracias por*
> *Bless Me, Última y todo) . . .*
> *Jemez Springs, New Mexico, July 2001*

creation

I journey with a magician
who points to the ocean,
"Without death there is no life."
This truth fills me with such

gratitude, I wake, heart
pounding with happiness,
not sorrow, happiness.
The magic of creation.

Dream, Chaco Canyon, August 2001

twenty crows

When the shadow of things
becomes more real than sunlight,
green branches dangling over
sidewalks, grass, then I

know the world has tipped just
enough for me to enter
truth   beauty   wonder—
there was a time when this

terrified me, seized me with
fear, now I feel the shadows
greet me, laughing, stretching
in sunlight   in moonlight—

I hear, "We are more real than
mountains, rivers, oceans, magma,
we are Keepers of the Dream, what
lives for-ever beyond the Light, we

are the world, the universe
you create when you close
your eyes to light, enter darkness,
guided by an *inner sun*

inner moon   you dream
falling stars, pastpresentfuture,
every thing is revealed,
no thing is revealed . . ."

I look up as twenty or so
crows circle in the hot
August air, their shadows
cool and silent, playing

freely
on this
perfect
planet. Now.

Longmont, Colorado, August 2001
(My son) Marc's home, front porch

wind horse

You lead me to Three Lakes,
three gifts, three sisters—
Onyx, Opal, Crystal—
up a narrow dirt-rock road

we bump and laugh, grow
silent as perfect beauty appears
all around all around all around
us—we hike to Crystal,

separate into silence, wind, swim
as eagles sing—we come together
to talk and laugh, speak our
separate lives, together—mothers

of children, lovers of men, we are
    (as night claims us) mother, daughter,
sister, friend, we are two women balancing
terror (worldwide rape of women, children, our

planet), and wonder (this moment as Venus flares
    hot and passionate, the dreams she brings,
Her Gifts)—we are two women sharing
timelessness in the first year of the next

1,000 planetary ones, and we do our
best to love this life, this world,
imperfect with sorrow, grief, loss
(our own, those swept up in

    wars, unspeakable childhood stories
we witness because we love the
    other)—we share this journey from
the joy-full back of Wind Horse,

the un-ending ride of those who
dare to marry loss and love, grief and

bliss, birth and death, male and female—
we ride oh we ride. We ride

through fear (our own, the others')
to fear less ness
to say the simple words   I   love   you
to dare to ride. This joy.

> *A la Adelita,*
> *amiga, hija, hermana—*
> *Sierra Madres, August 2001*
> *amor y milagros siempre jamás . . .*

blessing

I journey to sacred earth
   (though all earth is
sacred), this earth
begins healing to one

who arrives, kneels, scoops
from a small earth circle,
surrounded by Christian-Indian magic,
I place my offering behind the brown

skinned Goddess, tall as
a two-year-old—I feel this
peace that comes from the
Earth her self, I say,

"Heal my body, heal my heart,
heal my life, heal my family,
heal my world, let me travel
the world that I may see,

that I may see her beauty,
heal my body, healing Earth . . ."
All night lightning flashed, thunder
roared, their child *rain,* newly

born, arrived to dance and sing—
I placed the healing earth in
newborn shoes, as the child
rained down. On me.

Chimayó's earth, New Mexico
August 2001

> There are two ways to go to the gas chamber,
> free or not free.
> —Jean-Paul Sartre

soft chaos

I tie my fractured toe to the toe
next to it—after 8 planes, crazy Bali
traffic, 2 lanes become 3, 4, even 5, 6,
as motorcycles pass on both sides

(I break my toe right in my own front room) . . .

when I saw this mess, babies and children,
with no helmets, on motorcycles with their
parents, I was horrified—7 days later
I climbed on the back of a motorcycle

driven by a woman who'd just given me a
heavenly massage for $4 ($10 tip), her 4-year-old
daughter in front of her, me in a sarong, all of us
no helmets, young Balinese men yelling,

"Mama mia!" as we zipped by, my sarong
flapping in the sensuous breeze, at the
corner we're almost hit by a bus, no one
gets angry, upset (no problem), I'm

left wondering if my mangled body
would be cremated here with a grand
ceremony, or shipped back through
customs like stray baggage—then, I think

of all the people at the World Trade Center
falling   falling   falling   flying,   their final
choice, moments of freedom, rather than
wait like a prisoner for the fire to

eat them alive—I wept every
time they played it on CNN, now

I understand, I truly understand
their brief flight (I think I always

    did), but to have seen them
fall   fall   fall   fly   changed some
thing in me, some thing that felt safe, certain,
orderly. Now, I must embrace the

soft chaos,
brief moments
of freedom,
trust.

Bali, October 2001

gift

On Thanksgiving Day, my 35-year-old son,
his girlfriend, and I go shopping
for beauty and for food—
on the way to the car, in the

chill, it will snow soon here in
Santa Fe (in fact, it now snows
    as I write)—I'm stopped by
someone with jewels in his hands—

he extends them to me, "I'm selling these,"
he says. I look into his eyes,
I see the pain he was born into,
Indian, drunk, nose running, eyes

seeking mine, he says slowly, "My birth
day's tomorrow, my mother's dead."
I reach into my wallet, give him money,
wish him a happy birthday, refuse

to take his jewels—he tells me again,
"My birthday's tomorrow, my mother's
dead." I meet his eyes, "Yes, I understand,
but happy birthday anyway,"

I touch his shoulder, his worn out
coat, turn to enter the car where
my son, his girlfriend wait.
"Here, take these," he stops me.

"No, I can't take them, but
thank you."
"Here, you take them."
I'm left holding the jewels

as he walks away slowly—
maybe, I think, maybe
this was his birthday present,
to give something away.

Santa Fe, November 2001

MY INFINITY

my infinity

A wise woman and I stand
under the stars, I ask,
"Do they dance for you?"

"They make me laugh," she
says. "Look at the ones
swirling in red, I love those,"

I say. She leaves . . .
I'm never alone with the sky,
stars, my infinity.

Dream

lotus

Spring to winter to spring,
that's me—
behold my naked branches
just beginning to birth small

leaves, small flowers—
behold my feet and knees,
how they dance at every
turn, turn, turning—

behold my hands as I hold
sunlight tenderly, and
behold my eyes that love
the star at night through

my shut window, and
behold, oh behold, my
womb, heart, mind, they
open. Each one. A lotus.

*   *   *

This flower blooms in
every season, in the
ground of gratitude/betrayal,
from the ocean of sorrow/ecstasy,

from the sky of bliss/loss—
this flower blooms once in
a lifetime—this flower never
ever dies. Behold.

*   *   *

In the woman's hot tub,
each woman's body holds
the lotus,
the mystery—

spiraling snakes on one thigh,
coiled snake on small of back,
flower necklace, rose on shoulder,
butterfly on ankle, lotus with fire

rising sacrum, maze on shoulder, large
beautiful feathers forever on calf of leg,
and every woman present—
maidens, mothers, crones—

such ripeness, each stage,
the sensuality that grandmother
holds, her smile that says,
Behold this flower that never

ever dies.

Ten Thousand Waves,
Santa Fe, February 2002

wisdom

Snow on soft rounded cliffs
shaped like Spider Woman's
endless body, a small white-tipped
owl sings to me as I float in

a circle of sun,
hot sun,
silky sun,
healing sun,

you hold me in your ancient arms, I
am your daughter, I am your
dancing daughter in the circle of your
sun, sky, snow, ice, and the singing

small white-tipped owl—I am
the daughter who was born to
dance in the center of the sun, to
the rhythm of Her Heart.

Spin me,
sing me,
heal me,
once again—

you know the way of this journey,
each time I must *choose* my
innocence or die a fool—each time
I must weave the web of my own fragile

wisdom.

Dreams, omens, Venus—
Ojo Caliente, hot springs, February 2002

perfection

I see winter and spring,
sun and snow, marry
the other in the swirling
sky—

I stop to greet the
mystery—I stop to witness
magic as they unfold,
reveal themselves on this

ordinary day in March—
I see sun and snow
blessing every thing on this
ordinary Earth as war and peace,

good and evil, birth and
death continue to marry
the other, and I am
grateful. To see this

ordinary marriage
of mystery, magic
as all suffering,
all joy. Continues.

Blessed, moment
by moment
by moment.
Perfection.

*   *   *

Oh Spring   Oh Spring   Oh Spring   Oh Spring
I love you, more
than winter, summer, fall—
you are the newborn I can't

resist, you come through the
green, wet, fertile world of
birth—you come from the
silent, gentle, patient world of

death, carried by the soft,
so strong, enduring (enduring), green
hands of Earth, blue hands of Sea,
red hands of Fire, violet hands of

Sky—you are the newborn, you
are the newborn no one can resist,
ancestor (death), child (birth)—
O Child, our Child.

Perfection.

*   *   *

May you live in this world,
in all worlds, forever—
may you live in this cosmos,
in every cosmos, born, not
    yet born, forever—
May you live beyond human
    memory, dream, desire, born
always in the spring,
may it be so . . .
Perfection

Santa Fe, March 2002

voices

Guided by voices
—bumper sticker

I dream a young man standing in
the center of a sacred mandala,
shouting prayers to the Cosmos,
turning east, south, west, north,

he shouts and laughs though
bystanders think he's crazy,
he continues to sing his prayers to
the Cosmos loudly—the sacred mandala

is surrounded by ancient fire as women,
young children, enter to sing their
prayers loudly to the Cosmos—
then it's my turn to enter the ancient

fire and sing, and as I do the ancient
fire leaps and laughs, as I join the
choir of voices we hear all our
lives. If we listen.

*   *   *

If we're brave enough, crazy enough,
to crave the Ancient Fire, Sun, Moon,
Stars, Spiral of Creation, the Cosmos
where each voice is heard

and gathered into a bouquet of songs
never ever heard until this
moment if we listen, mouth open,
one voice. I hear.

*   *   *

"You will love me
more than any love
thus far, your
youthful loves pale,

preparation for
this time,
this love, listen well,
the center, Ancient Fire."

April 2002

orgasmic

(My Body)

My feet love me, take me
everywhere, dancing, to see
the world, to stand,
to stand in awe.

My legs love me, follow
my feet everywhere, dancing,
twin fiery horses, moving
just for joy, for joy.

My thighs love me, soft slopes
of the moon, the sun has
also kissed them, stroked them,
my moon/sun thighs.

My womb and vulva love me, hidden
fruit, no sweeter fruit anywhere,
woman of words and children, I taste
the fruit in dreams.

My ass and fluid spine love me, revealed
always revealed to light, the lotus
at the small of my back, small tongues
of fire and ecstasy.

My breasts and shoulders love me, young
girl's breasts at 57 and shoulders
of a boy, I delight in the girl,
the boy, my body.

My neck and head love me, one
wise, one curious, "Don't look"
"Look now"—wise and curious, old
and young, *look now.*

My hair loves me, curling toward my
eyes, nose, mouth, ears—all this fragility

loves me, I who will outlive it. This
body that loves the soul, my body.

*   *   *

(My Pearl)

In the center of my womb is a
perfect pearl, where children once
grew in the softness of my womb, a
perfect pearl—

and this pearl sings to the moon and
stars, sun and clouds, body and
soul—this is the Pearl of Perfect
Pleasure, treasure (of my body)—

this pearl, my pearl,
this treasure, my pleasure
loves me, this fragility
I am (and more)—

my tender womb loving all
the world, all children,
the Cosmos, holds her
orgasmic wisdom (my pearl).

Santa Fe, May 2002

(just joy)

Morning walk. Dolphins.
Human response. We're
seized by joy, not
rational, just joy.

The woman next to me
cries, "Oh look, the
dolphins!" Their
darkness sweet in

first sun. They
spin, hunt for food,
dance in air, breathe,
hunt, hunt, hunt,

as I hunt for joy
moment by moment by
moment. This life, esta
vida, has enough

necessary sorrows, the
ones that make us fully
human, capable of
l-o-v-e, so when

joy suddenly surfaces,
dark and sweet, not rational,
never ever rational, let it
wash over you, breathe it

in moment by moment by
moment. Let the dolphin,
joy, call you by name,
and may you answer

in the clear voice
of the Ancient Child,

"Oh look, the
dolphins, *oh look!*"

*   *   *

As I slowly walk the
beach, transfixed, they
surface, breathe, dance,
vanish, following them

down the beach, south,
coastal edge, I forget
who's swimming,
who's walking,

who's floating, spinning,
who's skimming gravity—
I forget to be human
for the longest time,

the dolphins' gift,
the ocean's gift.
Gift. Of the dreaming
child. Just joy.

Venice Beach, June 2002

her laughter

The Goddess laughs,
she sends me young men
in their twenties, most
recently a beautiful

lifeguard, a young
writer, at Venice Beach,
with blood of the Inca
he said, Peruvian,

about the age of my
youngest child, son—
I tell him I'm a
writer, we talk about

the novel, short stories,
dialogue and character,
he tells me he loves
to dance, I blurt,

I love to dance, we laugh,
I say I'm going swimming
in the Great Mother
   (I don't say

Great Mother, but
think it), he loves Her,
I see it in his eyes,
then he sees dolphins,

laughs and points
them out to me, he
tells me how a group
comes to greet him every

morning, stop, leap, swim on—
later he says, "We could go

dancing at this place called
The Temple . . ." I tell him

about my two sons
21, 35, but don't
tell him about my
21-year-old granddaughter—

"I'm serious," he says,
"there's some good music . . ."
"Well, I could go as
your friend maybe . . ."

"Mucho gusto, Alma," he
touches his heart, I touch
mine, we laugh, yes oh
yes,

the
Goddess
laughs
and laughs.

Venice Beach, June 2002

sacred feathers

Eagle Man, who I've known
for twenty-one years
and seven months (in my
womb, how you sang

to me your eagle songs,
kept me company in the
Sky of Creation)—in our
time, you are the rare

man, the one who loves
women, men, humans
without fear or shame—
I proudly walk with you

on Venice Boardwalk, stopping
to hear poetry, song, the sexy
couple dancing in a store
front window, blonde and

black, they enjoy each
other's bodies, we
look at each other, smile—
no fear, no shame, this

dance. I sit with you as
you receive your first
tattoo, two perfect eagle
feathers dancing in the wind,

symbol of balance and
wholeness, held in deep
red, clasps the feathers—
years ago I dreamt an

old, wise Yaqui in the
Sonoran Desert, he gave

me two perfect eagle
feathers, one female,

one male, he said, "Daughter,
fly toward our Sun, our
endless joy, remember the ice
but don't dwell there."

Take your Grandfather's
words, the feathers you
plucked from his dream,
may they guide you on

your journey in your, yes,
delicious body, may you
always fly in the Sky of
Creation toward the Sun,

may you always remember
you are loved, feel
my words in the wind,
your left shoulder. Fly.

A mi hijo, el Jules—
Venice, California, July 2002

welcome home

Jim,
this morning the news you
were struck by a hit
and run driver, you,

old friend, first editor
and publisher of my work,
my poems, your long
letter to me after I sent

you 20 or so, I remember
your generous words,
"Welcome, great poet,"
and you insisted I send

everything I had, our
correspondence, your
first visit to my farm
in Sonoma County, you

played jacks with my
13-year-old daughter and
fought for real to win, you
played every kid game with

my four boys—archery, ping-pong,
touch football, baseball,
hide-and-go-seek at the
beach after the barbeque

when it got dark and we
couldn't find you at all,
when it was time to leave
every voice yelling, "JIM"!

"HEY, JIM!" We were in
the Volkswagen bus, motor
started, when you jumped in
laughing like a madman,

"Where the hell were you,
Jim?" 8-year-old Marc yelled—
suddenly serious, "Well, I
was out there hiding, and I

think I hid too damned
good 'cause I turned into
a bear . . ." "A WHAT?"
all the kids screamed,

"A WHAT?" Then the
laugh, the madman's laugh,
the child's laugh, and suddenly
4 boys became bear cubs

jumping you, growling, you
laughed harder till you wept—
that's what it feels like,
Jim, you've become some

thing else, some thing so
wonderful, so magical, so
free, you have to hide,
to hear all our voices

calling you, urging you
to dance one more dance,
the dance of the laughing,
beloved bear, Jim.

(Welcome, old friend,
welcome, sweet poet,
welcome, tired traveler,
welcome home.)

To James Marion Cody, July 30, 2002—
friend and fellow poet for 30 years,
con todo amor,
Alma Luz Villanueva

secret

(to Frida Kahlo)

Four years before my
birth you painted your
self wounded, thorns
around your soft neck,

a live, dark bird
hanging from your
throat, blood on
your throat, calm

sorrow in your eyes,
a hungry cat on your
left shoulder, playful
monkey on your right.

You, Frida, staring out
at the world with pale violet
butterflies in your hair,
winged orchids in mid-air.

Sixty-two years later,
I surround your image
with healing hearts, sun,
moons, swans, male/female

death, a singing deer with
golden antlers—I hear
you singing, Frida, our
mysterious, healing

secret. To love in
spite of pain. To create
in spite of pain. To dance
in spite of pain. And

to live because of
joy, the live, dark
bird, the pale violet
butterflies, winged orchids.

To live
oh to live
in spite of
and because

of our mysterious,
healing secret
pleasure pain pleasure.
To sing.

Santa Fe, July 2002

Kata

"When surrounded by
the enemy," my kung fu
teacher said, "use the
Kata." She showed us

fluid striking movements in
the four directions—
"You are moving, your
center, your mind is

still," she'd smile,
then back to crippling,
killing blows, how I
loved this woman, June

Gong, barely five feet,
fingertip push-ups, blows
to solar plexus by very
large men, her WWHHOOOO,

her laugh. "This is a dance,
the dance of your spirit,"
she said, "stay in the
center, fear no one, not

even death, just dance,
just dance when you are
surrounded by the enemy . . ."
I remember the Kata,

practice it, arms, fists,
legs, body turning like
a sunflower to the
great Sun—even when

I'm very still, my spirit
dances. The Kata.

In the small human places
where we sit contained, being

civilized, my spirit
dances. The Kata.
When surrounded by
the enemy dance,

fear no one, not even
death. Dance and laugh
always laugh, center sun still,
turn, oh turn. To the great

Sun.

kill

Yes, I sleep with my
buck knife next to me,
slightly unsheathed, ready
for use, my kung fu

training . . . in the belly,
both hands, rip up,
in the neck, the center,
slice all breath, no

stabbing for me but
killing blows (if ever
      if ever)—please know
I do not (ever) wish

to kill anyone, no
I do not wish, but
I was once a seven-year-
old girl who was kidnapped

for some hours, not raped
but touched all over—
I was not killed, but
threatened to be killed if

I told, and I told, yes,
I told, and my kung fu
teacher, June Gong, barely
five feet, taught me killing

blows for a week,
just she and I, "You and
I, we are eagles," she
said laughing, correcting

my hands to better push
bone into brain. I watched
her square off with a muscled
man 6'3" and win, take full

throttle blows to her solar
plexus, her warrior yell
raising every hair, she stood
firm, laughing.

June, you were trained to
be a warrior at five by
your father in China,
you a girl, a woman who

would never ever marry you
said, "Women then become
slaves," you hissed, so serious
I thought you'd cry, then

your warrior's laugh—
Oh June, I do not wish to
kill, but if by killing those
two men . . . five- and six-year-

old bodies found, one still
missing . . . those girls would've
lived, yes I would kill
yes I would—

I who treasure life, have
created life in my womb four
times, I who have loved
men, my beautiful sons,

I would kill, June,
and so would you, just
to thank you, June,
your warrior's laugh.

August 2002

ENERGY

energy

I wear a wolf hat with a tail—
I laugh because I love it so
much—a man friend (who also
   wears one) laughs with me.

An older man approaches—he wants
to teach me something—I resist.
As I speak, pointing to my abdomen,
my womb, he says, "It's so beautiful

in there, isn't it?" "Yes," I say. "Is it
possible for the outside to be as beautiful
as the inside?" He laughs with delight—
"You can do it, it's possible, you can

do it, my child."
His smile, his laughter, his words,
give me confidence, the energy
I need to create the world in the

image of my womb.

Dream

bless me

Eagle staff, real eagle
head at tip, eagle
feathers, nine, sway
in the wind—

dancers, drummers, flute
players, singers, storytellers
gather under shady Mother
Tree—I come

to watch Rainbow Children
dance, each child holds
a rainbow in their hands—
I come to watch Corn Mother,

Father Sky dance, I come
to watch old warriors
dance, blankets on their
proud shoulders, I come

to watch young women
kick dust, twirl their beauty,
I come to watch the hunter's
myth, young man's hunger,

I come to watch young
boy eagles touch white wings
to Earth and Sky—
I come to hear of

Crazy Horse and Geronimo,
the spirits beyond count,
warrior men and women,
who come to perch this

day in the Mother Tree,
giving shade and wisdom,

ancient joy and anger,
tears and laughter, two

white feathers I pluck
from the ground below
eagle staff, eagle head,
bless me. Bless me.

*   *   *

Flute player, fancy dancer,
tells the crowd, "Welcome,
we aren't the *hostiles*"
(laughter)—then he asks,

"Any Navajos here? (Voices
say "Yes.") "Any Pueblo
here?" (More voices)—he
names more tribes and finally

Yaqui (My one voice, "Yes"),
he smiles at me, "Gotta
Yaqui here." He blows the
eagle bone so high,

so sweet, I remember
my grandmother's eagle eyes as
she gathered small stones that
day when kids started yelling,

"Dirty Indian!" Handed me
some, then eagle-eyed,
crazy-eyed, she threw
them as they scattered in

the wind—later she said,
"Our people are undefeated,

the Yaqui have never been
defeated," this in Spanish,

the Yaqui her own secret
language I never learned,
soft like prayer. As the
flute player and the drummers

play, shuffling grandfather, his
five-year-old grandson dance,
Plains Indians, undefeated this
day, grandfather trembling before

the eagle staff, grandson dancing
the ancient steps of the
Sun, bless us all,
us humans.

Santa Fe Plaza, August 2002

naked traveler

Facing the sky, I'm
as naked as the twilight
I was born—
the clouds are perfect,

what can I say—
the wind is also
perfect, as is the
setting sun, the

twilight that reveals
itself forever. In this
airport chair, I wait
to climb the sky

with man-made wings—
a small spider plant
shoots forth white
spring blossoms at

the end of a scorching
summer—a teenaged
boy a few rows to my
left sings in various

voices, whistles to the
music in his ears, he
reminds me of my sons
at that age, wholly

themselves and fuck the
world, that very young
spirit that *knows* it'll
conquer the world—

and I'm so naked
facing this wide expanse

of perfect sky—
here's my poem, my

song, my whistle, my
undiminished spirit that
has not conquered the
world, that will never

conquer the world, oh
but I live,
I whistle.
Fuck it.

        *   *   *

And what is the song
of the spirit?
What tune do
I whistle?

Am I as naked as
the twilight I was
born? Do I climb
the sky with joy or

fear? We are all that
teenage boy/girl wholly
in love with our wings,
our lovely, dreaming,

silver/gold wings, if
only we'd sing, "Fuck it,
here I go—" O world,
O universe, here

comes one more
fearless child

unfurling her
perfect wings—

only through fear to
fearlessness do those
wings unfold,
our wounded/whole selves

to love, yes, once
again, to love the
naked sky, our lovely, dreaming,
silver/gold wings, our undiminished spirit.

Here comes
one more
fearless, naked
traveler. Fuck it.

Los Angeles to Lake Chapala, Mexico
September 2002

the door swings open . . .

Is this where the magic
door swings open?
This opening of Earth
and Sky?

The clouds that guard
the gates?
The pure white birds
that know

the time forever?
The cobblestone streets
that trip the foot, but
horses dance on?

The hungry dogs that
ask your name, what
brought you here, the
hungry dogs that gauge

your hungry spirit,
are these the dogs
that let you pass
or not?

*   *   *

A man my age greets
all on the bus, each
face, then, standing, begins
to play his guitar and sing

in spite of the lurching
dance that would
send me through the
window, he never holds

on to any thing as he plays
and sings . . . Is this the
key to the magic door,
to not hold on to any

thing, to play your
guitar, to sing in the
most joyful voice, of
every love

you've ever known,
and
not
hold on?

To Marianne, Casa Tres Leones,
Ajijic, Mexico, September 2002

thunder beings

> We wed ourselves to the Mystery, not to conquer it,
> or be conquered by it, but to greet it.
> —Innuit song

I realize there are so many
people who do not know how
to greet the sacred,
the Mystery, in daily life,

what's in front of them, the
sun or rain or snow,
shining, each (daily) miracle—
I walk through mysteries

of endless trees gone yellow,
ground covered in yellow,
sky filled with yellow,
yellow snow they drift through

yellow sun to yellow earth,
my eyes are yellow, my tongue,
my brain, my heart, every inch of me
yellow so yellow it takes all

my social training, the grown-up-
from-this-culture-me, to not go
twirling, singing yellow songs, letting
our great yellow sun sing through

my wide open smiling mouth, I just
turned 58, am I too old for this yellow
yellow oh so yellow urge,
I wonder, *no*, I answer, you

are entirely sun-held, beauty-held,
sky-held, Earth-held, October-held,
moon-and-star-held, scent-from-the-
forest-floor-held, light-filled-creek-held,

so-cold-it-wakes-you-up-held,
one-stranger-beams-his-joy-to-
me-held, the-others-can't-help-
their-joy-held this yellow yellow day,

I greet the Mystery, old friend
from my child-girlhood, who
told me secrets, sent me dreams,
kept me child bride to its

languorous smile, wild leaps
roof to roof, the frightening
beautiful nights when pointy
stars pierced my tender skin,

and I sang to Thunder Beings—
now I think of the Thunder Being Bird,
14-foot wing span, seen in the north,
men say it looks like a small

plane, Keep your children in they say, keep
your children in, yet I know their children's
yellow dreams see it gliding over the
melting blue-white-hearted

nests of the Thunder Beings,
the melting
blue-white-hearted
glaciers.

Bandelier, New Mexico, October 2002

(prayer at 5 am)

The waning full moon wakes me
up, makes me look at 5 a.m.
through my black lace shawl,
it's so white and clear through

lacy late October leaves, my black
lace shawl, moonlight caresses
me, Wake up wake up, she moans
through my black lace shawl,

and I'm glad she woke me up, the
dreams of violence, not my own,
but the time, the world we live
in, a time of war, global war,

when humans find their way to peace
through war, the killing of each other,
mother, father, sister, brother, all our
relatives, all our relatives, when

humans inch their bloody path
        one planet   one people
all our relatives   all our relatives . . .
she wakes me up to give me hope,

just a glimpse of her wiselight,
one pale star
still visible
so high,

I see this new century,
bloody with love and horror,
it's not the century I wish to
give to my children, grandchildren,

their children, all children,
but it is the century we're

called to create, together, the
waning full moon tells me, and

the one pale star
still visible
so high
over us. All.

All our relatives
all our relatives
all our
relatives. All.

October 25, 2002, Santa Fe, New Mexico

"fear not, my child"

Day of gold, we walk, my
friend and I, toward the Great
Ceremonial Kiva in Bandelier,
Spider Woman in the form of

Dancing Tarantula, black graceful
legs, dances our path, so we
squat and stare and breathe
her sacredness, this dancing

Spider Woman at the edge of
winter greets us, so, yes, we squat
and stare and breathe in deeply her
sacredness, how she creates our world,

our universe and every cosmos, every sun
that ever was, ever will be, tears fill
our eyes as we continue, we worry,
our world on the usual brink of

war, the end of our species, the
unfolding beauty of our children,
all children, their promise given to them,
by, yes, Spider Woman, as I promised each

of my children portions of joy, hope, always
love, woven with strands of tears, sorrow,
always transformation in the guise of
grief, always Spider Woman's unending

weaving, unending beauty, terror, wonder . . .
we climb ladders straight up from forest
floor, the creek that sings of light,
thirst, life, ancestors who carried

water up this cliff, their ancient
ladders, we climb without carrying

water, then separate to sit, stare,
breathe in the sacred—a large

Pueblo man climbs with no effort,
as though these steep ladders were only
stairs no fear no fear of Earth or Sky,
he climbs, enters the Kiva, down the

ladder, begins to sing Spider Woman's
song of Earth weaving Sky, of darkness
weaving light, of winter weaving spring,
of spring weaving summer, of death

weaving life, of dreams weaving us
humans for ever, ever, in this Galaxy,
in this Sun, in every galaxy that ever
was, or ever will be, she dreams us into

being, he sings from the center of the
Earth . . . Spider Woman whispers in
the wind, *Fear not, my child, fear not
my child, you are all that ever was,*

*you are all that ever will
be, fear not, my child, my weaving
is without end, you are all that ever was,
ever will be, oh Beauty . . .*

*   *   *

Circling the Kiva:
We climb down the
ladder, hands on walls, we
circle the Kiva, voices mingling:

"All our relatives, peace for us on Earth, all,
all our relatives, peace for us on Earth, all . . ."

we circle one way, we circle the other way,
singing so sweetly, Ancestor Wind

hears us,
pauses, stares,
breathes us in,
breathes us out, sacredly . . .

*   *   *

Later: Cliff walls that pulled
me here from ocean in dreams, each
night I flew, stared, breathed in the
sacred, dreaming these walls:

spiral suns, dancing animals, dancing
people, dancing birds, dancing dreams,
all our ancestors, all who ever were,
all who ever will be, they return,

I return to these cliff walls: slithering
slow slow diamondback rattler, we watch
Grandmother/Grandfather Snake glide slowly
toward dreams, winter dreams to spring sun:

Guardian of the Dream,
Guardian of these cliffs, when I come
in dreams this winter, remember me,
Great Dreamer, my ancient child's heart . . .

*   *   *

The Wind . . .
We are all
that ever was,
we are all
that ever will

be, we are
at the center
of the universe,
fear not, fear not, my child . . .

To Adelita, Bandelier, New Mexico
(and to the Pueblo man who sang his
ancient song in the Great Ceremonial Kiva),
between the worlds, October 31, 2002

sun song

Love the sunflower,
it gives you yellow, hope
and fleshy seeds—it teaches
you how to turn toward

the sun each day, to seek
its warmth and wisdom—
yes, love the sunflower,
each perfect petal, soft

as baby toes, its wide brown
face where seeds ripen, and
broad generous green so green
leaves, hands that move in

the wind as the sunflower
turns and dances, face offered
up to the sun, dances and turns.
Love the sun . . .

Santa Fe, November 2002

skin

> Just as a snake sheds its skin, we must shed our
> past over and over again.
> —Buddha

Now I drink my wine
from a crystal glass,
the ones I used to save
for guests, and yes

the wine tastes better in
crystal—now I buy
flowers no one else sees,
only I see their beauty,

unfolding—now I buy
beauty for my walls and
only I gaze day in day
out—now I buy new

music and only I listen
with joy, only I dance
toward evening—now I
buy things to wear that

make me happy or sad
or comfortable in my own
skin—now my skin
belongs to me, such lovely

skin that covers strong
bones from weight lifting,
push-ups—now my soul
knows its own song,

that delicate balance between
joy and grief,
pleasure and pain,
the endless letting go,

someday, of this body,
this endlessly curious body,
in love with every thing my
soul can touch,

we touch like babies
discovering our own
delicious skin for
the first time.

        *   *   *

I have become
newly born, maybe
eight months old,
my feet fascinate

me for hours, and
my hands, these butterflies
that glide over my baby
head, some times I eat

them, some times I eat
my feet—I forget,
absolutely, all the other
births, when Light first

created me, I created
light from womb
darkness, no evil, no,
no evil, just LIVE—

I forget my roles of
mother, daughter, wife, always
lover, and if I was ever a
man I truly forget, my

body, skin, cells, have
no male memory, only

female remains, the body,
I mean, the baby.

*   *   *

Goodbye, sweet skin, you
glitter by moonlight as
I glide, slide, newly
born at 57, how

I love my new sweet
skin, how I love
my new life, this new
toy. Now. I play.

Now   I   play
Now   I   play
Now   I   create
words   love   oh   skin . . .

mi alma/my soul

I feel like Pancho Villa when
he said upon seeing
la mar, "Not enough
water to quench my

thirst." I feel this
thirst at 58, wide,
deep, sensuous and
stormy as the constant

tide, I want to swell,
heave, roll, swell to
spill continent to
continent, I want my

thirst never (ever) to be
quenched, I want to be
the one small wave in
the endless

sea, to kiss one
shore then the other
and the other for ever
and ever, my one small

wave, tidal hand, touching
earth, birthing dolphins,
cycles of moon, stars,
sun in my moving, living

mirror, my living, sparkling
mirror. I want to be the woman
with seashells in her ears,
listening—I want to be the woman

who dies thirsty for more,
grateful for every sip,

every breath, the one
small wave. I am.

＊　　　＊　　　＊

I will wear sparkles on
my cheeks, eyelids, lips,
neck, exposed flesh—
I will sparkle in my 58th

year like the moving, living
ocean, her beauty in
the Great Sun's light,
sparkling—she sparkles

in spite of killing sonar waves,
in spite of world wide
pollution of her great
waters, in spite of

extinction of her ocean
children, in spite of
the ingratitude of her
earthly children, she

continues to sparkle with
light and joy, she continues
to sparkle, as I will
continue to sparkle with

store bought glitter, and the
light I borrow from the
Great Suns, for ever, this
sparkling joy, mi alma.

From San Antonio to Santa Fe, November 2002

SPIRIT SONG

spirit song

As I walk in a beautiful
place on this Earth
I sing my Spirit Song—
no words, only music—

and my heart is so open—
and my heart is so joyful—
that I have walked this far
in beauty.

Dream

dear world,
dear, dear Ixchel,

I must tell you some
thing wonder full, one
small miracle in the
world, a speck of dust in

the cosmos . . . but what a
glittering, luminescent speck of
dust . . . in a tiny country called
Bhutan (one side China,

the other India, like
sacred Tibet, her people,
invaded by once wise China) . . .
in Bhutan, their leaders speak of

"Gross National Happiness"—
everyone farms, no hunger—
everyone schooled, no ignorance—
everyone health care, no despair—

no hunger, ignorance, despair
of the *forgotten poor*—
everyone wears the timeless
clothing of their ancestors, meant

to not distinguish the king
from the farmer—and
the king's four wives,
four sisters, rule the

kingdom, four goddesses to
his god, to the gods and
goddesses who reside in
the farmer, the seamstress,

the weaver, the poet . . .
"*Namaste,* I honor the
Goddess, the God in
you" . . . the Bhutan leader

who speaks to the reporter on
my TV says they've finally
brought TV to Bhutan, to honor
the global village we've become,

our speck in the cosmos,
our glittering, luminescent
jewel called Earth—
they know the danger

but trust in the
Goddess, the God that
resides in the strangers, in
me, in us *Namaste* . . . finally, we're

shown their mountains, the
highest in the region . . .
when the Goddess and God,
masquerading as the farmers

and shepherds, who live at
the feet of their mountains,
complained, didn't want their
sacred mountains scaled,

"conquered" by climbers, their
leaders upheld their truths,
their dreams, their visions
their mountains are sacred,

no conquerors for their silent
sacred Mystery. I pray

they will assimilate us—
I pray our TV entertains

them, warns them,
teaches them our ways—
I pray I pray they are
strong enough to transform

us, this tiny country called
Bhutan, where the
major export is their
Gross National Happiness.

dear world,

In Tibet, under Chinese rule,
five Buddhist nuns would not
sing songs of Chinese praise
    (too many tortured, too many killed)—

instead, they shouted and sang,
"FREEDOM FOR TIBET, OUR PEOPLE,
FREEDOM TO PRAY TO CHANT TO SING,
FREEDOM TO FREEDOM TO FREEDOM TO LIVE . . ."

five Buddhist nuns would not sing, 50 years
and over one million dead—they were beaten with
wooden planks, belt buckles, rubber hoses filled
with sand, electric prods to their tongues their tongues,

ears and genitals, forced to stand in the hot hot sacred
sun for four days with a piece of paper between
their knees, a cup of water on their heads, still
they would not sing songs of Chinese praise—

and on the fifth day the five Buddhist nuns were
given time for personal needs, they took the
white white sacred scarves of prayer, of
song, stuffed them down their silent

throats . . . so, dear World, as Israeli
soldiers kill the twelve-year-old his father tried
desperately to shield, as the Palestinian teen
raises both hands with the Israeli soldier's blood,

I take pleasure, utter pleasure, in the
shouts, noise, songs of children taking
over the quiet pool with signs that
say SILENCE PLEASE . . .

or the elderly Mexican man in the
Wal-Mart parking lot who suddenly
begins to sing a song of love as
he pushes his shopping cart, I meet his

eyes and say, "Beautiful, your voice is
beautiful." He smiles with utter pleasure,
singing louder, more beautifully
of love.

Dear World,
thank you oh
thank you for
the singers.

dear world,

Will we humans violate the
Arctic wilderness, now,
for oil
for cars
for profit . . .
will we humans continue the
violation of this planet,
this place, this earthly
paradise,
dear World?

Polar bear dancing with
wolf dancing with
caribou dancing with
eagles dancing with
mice dancing with
seals dancing with
whales dancing with
ice dancing with
clouds dancing with
ozone dancing with
rain dancing with
Earth dancing with
humans dancing south
humans dancing east
humans dancing west
humans dancing north

will this paradise be lost,
dear world?

September 16, 2001
Karma means you don't get away with anything.
—Ruth Denison, Zen Master

dear Ixchel,

3,000 souls,
3,000 lights,
3,000 (and more) humans
lifted, flew, left our

Earth—each one, did
you hold their souls
hold their souls, dear
Ixchel?

Insane men take planes
full of people,
full of people,
turn their spirits into

bombs—as their souls
lifted, the people in the
World Trade Center, as
they   fell   fell   flew,

lifted, did the insane men's
souls, as they lifted,
as they lifted, did their
souls cry out, cry out

"What have I done,
what have I done . . ."
Did they cry out,
Ixchel?

Did they cry out in shame
and horror as the White
Light, your exquisite rainbow
wings, enclosed them in undying

157

love, as they understood, there
is no "hell" only re-birth and
re-birth until we get it right,
one planet, one people—

newborn babies, no sin,
only karma, life to be lived,
the whisper of your rainbow
wings, dear Ixchel.

February 5, 2002
Learn to let go. That is the key to happiness.
—Buddha

dear world,

The huge purple crystal on my
table reminds me of your presence—
complex, simple, breathing valleys
of quartz, staggering mountain tops

of light, sheer light, it reminds
me of how much I love to roam you,
wander you, love you, step by step—
in Venice, Italy, now, magical people

dressed in magical costumes celebrate
your wonder in their own wondrous
way (I want to join them, I want
    to join them, to wear a feather mask,

to wander with no personal history, who I've
been, who I am, who I'll be, I want
a butterfly wand to guide my way)—
in Bali people celebrate the wonder

daily, celebrate that our crystal
world spins on her perfect axis, tilting
always toward the Great Sun—yes,
I know there's great human suffering, yet

also equal (or more) the wonder—
in my fifty-seventh year, dear World,
I tilt myself to witness your
unbridled wonder,

this endless
journey
of joy.
I want to see.

I want to know.
I want to hold.
The world in my
arms.

I want to be.
The beloved in
love, and loved by
you, dear World.

dear world, dear Ixchel,

When Jesus said, "Let the
children come unto me,"
I know he meant to touch,
to hear, to know their

innocence—to touch, to hear,
to know a child's trust,
our teacher's on the path to
home, wonder, wisdom, the

great gift of innocence. Ixchel,
why do "holy men" take the
innocence of our children, why do
"holy men" take the wonder of our

children, and why do they maim the
souls of our children, Ixchel? Take
the sunrise and holy sunsets from
them, take the songs of birds from

them, take spring warmth and first
snowfall from them, take the
new and full moon, and especially
Venus, from them, take the oceans

(every dolphin, whale, spark of dancing
light) and the holy, sacred Earth
from them, take the healing winds
(south, west, north, east), the sky,

from them, take the scent of roses
from them, take the taste of honey
from them, take every memory of
comfort (if they have any), take it,

yes, take it from them, take your
healing presence from them, Ixchel
(Tara, Isis, Shing Moo, Kali, O Goddess)
protector of the Sacred Child. Then, maybe, maybe

they will know
what they took
from the
innocent.

To the unholy priests

dear world,

The sacred glaciers are melting,
the Sacred Sentries of the Earth,
melting,
pure ice, pure winter, pure renewal

and boundaries that hold
the Turtles, the humans,
in her firm embrace of
ice, winter, renewal, her

sacred boundaries,
begin to
melt,
begin to

melt—O Ixchel,
what will we do
without winter,
renewal, death?

dear world,
dear sky,
dear ocean,
yes, dear ocean,

Whales, dolphins, otters, seals,
all sacred life in your womb,
our womb, where we grew, we
humans, watery we were, and are

still mostly water, when we sit
by you, walk by you, swim
in you, yes we remember, Madre
Mar, Great Mother Ocean,

where all life began, begins
to begin, to be born for ever. In
my country USA men want to
drown your sacred heartbeat

with sonar, men who have forgotten
to listen to their own hearts,
the songs of whales, dolphins,
otters, seals, you Great Ocean

Womb—and if they drown your
Great Ocean Heart, Madre Mar,
if they maim and kill all life
in our womb, we will cease

to be human. If they drown your
Great Ocean Heart, we will be more
than orphans, we will be creatures
of terrible silence,

no heart
no home
no human
song.

NO SONAR, Mr. Bush,
Mr. Powell, Mr. England—
From all women, and men, who hear Her heart.
October 6, 2002

dear world, dear sweet earth,

I create spring in winter,
buy 10 tightly closed yellow
daffodils, place in clear
water, bathed in light at

7,000 feet. In dreams
they sing, "We are the
Ancient Spring, older than
flesh and blood—we are the

Ancient Spring, older than
the Sun, born of first
light, first darkness, yes,
we are the Ancient Spring,

older than your winter."
In the morning, one daffodil
opened its mouth and sang,
"I am here, yellow spring."

*　　*　　*

Dear Sweet Earth, they sang . . .

Daffodil #1, "I am here, yellow
spring, in time of sorrow, war,
lovers, joy . . . O joy to the lovers
who find love in winter's spring."

Daffodil #2, "I am here, yellow
spring, passed hand to hand, I
live in crowded cities, vast
deserts, by the salty sea."

Daffodil #3, "I am here, yellow
spring, brought to the dying child's

bed, she smiles wisely . . . *spring, rebirth . . .*
she laughs, the angel on the ceiling."

Daffodil #4, "I am here, yellow
spring, closed tight each bud, he brings
me to his sweetheart, he worries,
will I open for his love?"

Daffodil #5, "I am here, yellow
spring, brought home by a young
woman soldier to comfort her children,
to believe in spring, she prays silently."

Daffodil #6, "I am here, yellow
spring, quickly stolen by a girl
who wishes beauty on a snowy day in
Berlin, running, laughing, yellow joy."

Daffodil #7, "I am here, yellow
spring, a young man dreams in a field
surrounded by yellow yellow spring, dreaming
of his childhood before he goes to war, he weeps."

Daffodil #8, "I am here, yellow
spring, given to the new child, just
born, such innocence, new goddess/god
comes to visit this brand new yellow Earth."

Daffodil #9, "I am here, yellow
spring, every child, every where, holds
yellow in their ancient hearts, their ancient souls,
their brand new hands and eyes . . . they simply love."

Daffodil #10, "I am here, yellow
spring, the president of this country wants

to steal the world's spring, choose yellow,
in spite of, choose yellow spring. Love."

My country, the USA, brings war,
so-called "shock and awe," as the
sweet Earth turns yellow with spring—
To the people, all of us, March 2003

dear world
(dear Praveer),

You are ten years old in India—
you wind silk thread for looms
fourteen hours daily, every single day—
your fingers bleed—
your body slowly poisoned by color/dye—
you are only ten years old in India—
you can never play, you are beaten—
you can never dream your mother's smile—
you can never eat with happiness—
you wind silk thread for looms
fourteen hours daily, every single day—
your parents received $35 for your life—
you stare out at me—
you stare out at the world from
this photograph, next to bright red cloth,
the dye that poisons you daily, the
million other children, slaves like you,
Praveer, and I say to you, Praveer,
you are our child.

>   (Log onto www.nationalgeographic.com
>   for worldwide slavery information, ways
>   to protest this cruelty. Also, give to www.mercycorps.org,
>   a group that gives hope to children everywhere.)

dear world

(Dear Ixchel, because you tend the flowers),

Because a bright purple flower
with three small petals blooms
from a thin, pink tongue, semi
tropical plant, green spray of

hair from center, luxurious,
playful, secretive of its purple
flower, who would guess a flat,
thin, pink tongue would sing this

bloom, this flower? And because
this purple flower, just one, sings
so perfectly, I live one more second,
one more minute, one more hour, one more

day. On March 30, 2003, in Baghdad, a 14-year-old boy
was killed digging a trench in front of his family home—
U.S. bomb tore off the back of his head.
"He was a boy like a flower," his father said.

To Arkan Daif

dear world,

I want to hold the rainbow
in my hands, the rainbow
straight from the Sun—
I want to eat the rainbow,

be clothed by the rainbow,
a tropical bird in my 59th year—
I want to send the rainbow to
encircle you, dear World, to

keep you and all my relatives
safe—every human being tortured,
starved, killed, let the rainbow
comfort them with her spray of song.

250 million light years away, the Perseus
Cluster, a perfect, yes perfect, B-flat
note has been humming to Creation for billions
of years. And the rainbow, dear World.

When all the terrorists have homes, food
for their families—
when all the orphaned children of AIDS and
war are loved—

When women no longer fear violation,
rape, every two minutes in USA, in war,
globally, women's, children's bodies,
not sacred, always sacred—

When all the hunger every where becomes
wheat, corn, milk, wine—we will,

we will join the deep hum in perfect
pitch, B-flat, her spray of song, dear World,

dear planet, dear Sun,
dear humans, dear relatives,
dear Perseus Cluster, dear Galaxy,
dear rainbow wrapped Earth.

healing mercy

The small glassed-in Chinese pavilion
I bought in Chinatown, San Francisco,
years ago is no longer
glassed-in—its beautifully carved

wooden, tiny pavilion with two
white cranes is now open to
air, time, space, the song of
migrating birds, my heart in

flight, grounded in the present.
In my dreams, I see a wounded
goose in a roofless cage, then
healed into air, time, space, the

song of migrating birds.
My heart has no roof, only
sky, sun, moon, stars. This is
my song. No roof.

*   *   *

On my way to a reading in
Santa Barbara, I see a man in
his 80s, standing by the side of the
freeway exit, holding his baseball hat in

his hands, asking for
some thing, asking for
mercy, as we all must
drive on, no roof,

only sky
over all
of our
heads.

*   *   *

Buddhist practice, *tonglen:*
breathe the pain/sorrow in,
breathe the joy/healing out,
breathe our human pain in,

breathe our human joy out,
breathe our global sorrow in,
breathe our global healing out
to each other, each one, mercy.

As my country wages war in spring 2003

NO ROOF

no roof

I keep a wounded goose in
a roofless cage, she flaps
out of it, over and over,
then a young man opens

the door, she flies
free to blue sky, the sun,
I stand watching, no roof
over my head, free.

Dream

"Poetry should be in the ocean raining words slowly
onto fish."
  —from poems by fifth graders taped to a
  Venice wall, facing the Pacific

the wise wall

O Venice, sweet village of
maniacs, dreamers, poets, every
kind of human being, child poets,
parents, business people, gardeners,

waiters, filmmakers, actors, singers,
dancers, the homeless in every guise,
psychics, surfers, runners, skaters,
bikers, fish gathering words, gathering

words under rain, under sun, under moon, under
wave upon wave, the sudden dolphin
leaps up and up, spinning, dancing
in thin air, the poem . . .

O Venice, how could I not
love you as you hold the memories
of vanished poets; each time I
return, you remember me.

        "Poetry should be a sky with lots of
        glowing stars."

O Venice, star-filled, full
of moonlight, sunlight, poetrylight,
your sky of night dreams, day
dreams, whale dreams, pregnant

with their young and song dreams as
they journey to Baja, always the Arctic,

do stars guide their way?
Does poetry guide their way?

Do stars guide my/our way?
Does poetry guide my/our way?
As we journey north to south,
east to west, border to non-existent

border, poetry knows no borders,
only song and light to be shed,
every child's voice singing their
mother tongue, O Venice.

"Poetry should never stop in your dreams
where you are falling."

O falling, dreaming Venice,
you are as strange and beautiful
as a rainbow, sudden
rainbow on my wall, my open

hand, every child's eyes (be they
    newly born or the Ancient Child
who dreams us into being . . .)—how
the rainbow falls to Earth, how

in dreams we fall fall fall in the
last possible moment, our wet
rainbow wings spread wide, so
wide (suddenly) with joy (terror

    and wonder) and as we fall fall fall
to Earth like rainbows, suddenly we
fly into the sky of your dreaming,
O falling falling falling flying Venice.

> "Poetry should be the Sun warming
> your heart."

(Santa Fe, New Mexico)

I wear my new red leather boots, warm,
lined with sheepskin, to the Pueblo Deer
and Buffalo Dance—men bare-chested in
the morning air, chests and faces painted

black, the women with bare arms, drummers
and singers sing Sun-heart poetry to animal
spirits who guide our dreams, feed our bellies,
warm our feet—deer horns with white flying feathers,

buffalo horns with long swaying
red feathers, the hunters
with bow and arrow, the women
with shining knives, the singers

singing Sun-heart poetry, keeping dancers
warm, their singing Sun-hearts, these snowy
mountains, I stand in my red sheepskin boots,
knowing poetry shines on us all, each Sun-heart, O Venice.

> "Happiness sounds like an ocean
> in your ear."

I love my red boots,
red feet, my feet
that love to travel—
I stand in my red boots in

the Santa Fe sun, listening to
pearl-white-shell-music from

Bali, where I snorkeled nude,
dreaming, flying neon fish swimming

through me and through me, I actually
laughed underwater, mouth closed,
eyes open, oh the wonder of
being, dreaming, swimming, listening,

nakedly, to all the happiness in the
world, in the ocean, now
I stand here, red boots, this
perfection. In my ear. Facing you, O Venice.

> "Poetry should feel like some thing burning
> in side you that you just want to shout
> out loud."

O Venice, O California, O Mexico,
O this Continent, O Asia, O Europe,
O Spinning Planet, O Sacred Turtles,
I was born with this fire, and

I will die with this fire,
O Earth Star, the center of the Galaxy
is our home, I was born to sing
from the center of my fire,

and so if I sing and shout with all
the dead and living poets, with all
the true 5th grade poets every
where who know what I know . . .

this borderless Earth Star is our home,
One Planet   One People   One Fire
Let the children play, sing and shout
their burning, our truth, your ocean ear, O Venice.

> "Poetry should fly in the open sky and
> open new worlds."

O World, may our poetry make you
new, may we
create a new
world

as we sing this poetry daily,
may children remember they
were always sacred, they
are always sacred,

small gods and goddesses
the day they were born; in
Bali their young deities do not
touch the Earth, the new new

world, for four months—may we
remember who we are, who we truly
are, as we walk, dance, sing, the new world
into being (are you listening, my vagabond Venice?)

> "Poetry should be like oxygen so people
> could breathe it."

May the breath of the
world be full of poetry,
every language,
every country—

one planet
one people

May the winds of our
world bring poetry to

every tree, every flower,
every ocean, every human—

    one planet
    one people

May the sunlight of our
galaxy bring poetry to
every planet, every star,
every void, every dreamer—

    one planet
    one people

May the sky that holds
our moon, our stars, our
voices, be full of poetry raining
words slowly onto fish, us humans,

    one planet
    one people
    one fiery sun-heart
    one poetry-filled sky

Venice, California/Santa Fe, New Mexico
December 2002

vision quest

Live TV shows, people survive
in beautiful places for one million
dollars—people find the love
of their life in front of millions

of eyes, or don't—and people go
to war in front of billions of eyes,
our side, their side, everyone watches
The Shock and Awe Show brought to

us live from Baghdad, the faces of
the desperate, no food, no water,
terror in children's eyes as The Show
goes on and on and on as our young

soldiers die, their young soldiers die,
children's bodies, families carried from
the wreckage, what a show and it's *live*,
you couldn't pay to see this, that's it,

it's really the Freedom Show, we're
here to free them whether they like it or
not, whether it kills them in the
process, why one colonel even signed

a bomb personally (the news person
    said), now that's what I call the
personal touch, kind of like the surgeon
who signed that woman's womb, so very

thoughtful, why in four days we've sent them
$1 BILLION in cruise missiles, wisely not spending
the estimated 74 BILLION DOLLAR war package on
education, families without medical care, children who go

to sleep hungry in the Land of the Free, yes, *here,* and
those awful welfare mothers, no, not a cent . . .

I want, I want, oh, I want Mr. Bush (he's not
   my president) to go on a vision quest,

to fast for four days, four nights,
I want, oh I want him to feel the
hunger, thirst, fear and pain of the
world, yes, I want him to have

his very own vision quest, I want the
Great Spirit, Allah, Goddess, God
to give him the *real shock and awe*
of his life, cosmic truth, earthly truth,

human truth (not his little ego droning on
   and on), but *the truth* each human being
faces as they die, leave the body, not a
camera on them—for now, we watch

The Freedom Show Live, and maybe the wisdom is
this is our global vision quest, every one on their
mountain seeing all, world wide, at a glance, this
beautiful planet cradling us all to

the very end.

> As Bush tries to pass a 30 BILLION DOLLAR budget cut for
> veterans' funds, while he extols "the troops"—as our young
> men and women sacrifice their lives, and those who survive,
> our new war veterans, how dare he . . .
>   April 2003

graduation day and my purple hat . . .

I came in my purple
hat, figuring you'd
find me that way,
graduation day, thousands of people—

I came in my purple
hat because that's the
way you'd know me, the
woman with the purple hat—

I came in my purple
hat, simply because I'm
so proud of you, love you
from your sweet time in my womb—

I came in my purple hat,
thinking when you found me
in all the thousands we'd laugh,
I even stood on a chair like a giant orchid—

I came in my purple hat
and loved the way others also loved
their grown children, though someone
yelled, "Get off the fucking chair!" The Orchid glared,
sat down (people trying to stand in front me, on my sandaled
    feet)—

I came in my purple hat,
took photos of the throngs, some who continued to try to
steal my envied seat in the front row, some looking for their
graduating loved one, helium balloons poking sky in clusters
    (I'm here I'm here)—

I came in my purple hat, but
it didn't help, I just
couldn't find you, or you me,
on your graduation day, that's life—

But I tell you this: I am not
the mother of a young man
shot for walking down the street,
so many brown-skinned men

die like this—I am not
the mother of a young man
going to jail for 5, 10, 20
years, life—I am not the

mother of a young man
shot down, blown up in
Baghdad, ensuring our flow
of oil, thank Goddess, I'm

not the mother of these young
men, and thank God too—
I am the woman in the purple
hat, up at 4 a.m., journeyed in

one day (plane, rental car lines),
hours in the melting sun, finally
exhausted when I couldn't find you,
or you me, my purple hat

just a dot in the rainbow.
I should've stayed and melted,
I should've stayed and wilted,
but it's not my style, so I

left in a weird altered
state of sorrow-grief-total-exhaustion
that fluctuated with anger,
why didn't you confirm our

meeting place, if there
was one in that crazy

loving mob. Later
we spoke, and as you

joked, Try to see it in a
Buddhist slant, well okay—
I came in my purple hat
to be in that moment, in that

space, to wish you well,
to cheer you on, invisible
as an ancestor to your eyes,
firmly lodged in your heart

no matter where you go, old
age will find me there, the
woman in the purple hat
always singing, always shouting,

standing on a chair,
blooming in your
heart, congratulations
always. With love, Mom.

A mi hijo, Jules Villanueva-Castaño
UC Irvine, June 2003

chicha

My last full day in
Venice and the Wise
Voice tells me, "Go to
the Machu Picchu exhibit,

The Natural Museum."
But I want to spend my
last full day at the
beach, my toes squeezing

sand, the tide finding
my feet, ankles, thighs,
Lord Chaos building sand
castles that love the

air, sky, in perfect circles,
he builds—the drummers
up by Breeze Street on the
sand, the dancers rising to

move like undulating waves, the
waves in their ears with drums,
flute, rattles, sticks and song,
"Do you feel the Sun Gods?

Do you feel the symp-toms?" But
no, I take Venice Blvd all the
way and slowly, like a camera
rolling, Venice Beach turns into

Mexico, more and more Mexican
people, children, teens, families
on Venice Blvd, ice cream
vendors pushing carts, whole

juice vendors, families surround,
smile, talk, laugh, the weekend,

day of rest in Venice, Mexico—
signs in Spanish for *comida,*

ropa, herbs and charms for
limpias, I want to stop, go
in, but the Voice says,
"Machu Picchu, girl, stay

on track today . . ." Families
in the park by the museum,
Spanish in my ears every
where, the young man who

takes my parking fee, *gracias.* Inside,
dark museum, Why am I here?
I complain, then I see the
seven tiny gold (real gold, not

melted by the conquerors)
herons, I'm enthralled, the Sun
Gods in the gold, Mamaquilla
Earth Moon Goddess whispers,

"Welcome." The Ancient One in
my current novel smiles widely,
then laughs as I see the gold cup
he carries in his woven-rainbow

traveling pouch, the Inca bird
head, the two perfect ears of
golden corn woven on the
cup's back. I see him

pick it up to drink his
chicha, corn beer made by
women chewing, spitting,
fermenting—a young white

man disgusted by this process
says, "That's why they only lived
to twenty-five, dude."
Mamaquilla gleams through my

eyes and I tell him something I
don't even know, "No, they
actually lived into their fifties,"
and I add, "a beautiful life . . ."

He scowls, moves on, the final
panel, this section, says the chicha
was so healthy, they lived into their
fifties until the conquerors brought

measles, smallpox, plague, death
by sword and slavery.
The Ancient One, in my novel,
takes a deep sip of chicha from

his golden cup with bird
and woven corn, and 200 pages
or so into the novel I finally know
where he's from, but I still

don't know what he wants
to give me, he and the thirteen-
year-old Yaqui girl from Mexico,
the self-inflicted scar on her face,

her journey as a boy
north with this Inca, this
traveler, this trader who brings
the great Sun up with his eagle

flute. In my novel, in my dream,
they travel south to north, as I

travel Venice to Mexico in thirty
minutes or so. He and the young girl

(little grandmother, 400-1,000 years old)
laugh, refusing to tell me what's in
store, only that I must continue to
follow the dream (seven tiny perfect

    golden herons, all in a row,
wings outstretched for flight,
    escaped the fire, the golden
bird cup with woven golden

    corn for chicha, so good
for you)—only that I must
follow the novel, the dream,
to the very end,

the mysterious gift each novel
brings, each moment brings.
She chews, spits, ferments the
corn. He drinks.

                    Venice, Califas, Mexico, June 2003

sun gods

Summer Solstice, Venice Beach,
first the palm reader, an
older woman, kind eyes,
sees truth, sees the

words in my palm, sees
my children grown, travel,
some healthy selfishness
(at last, hooorrayy!!), and

that my writing will only
get better in this next phase,
I will write till I leave the
planet, and my life will be

long, and I've already
lived at least seven lives,
so I'm always ready to
die, each moment, now—

I face the sea, the sky,
the Sun, the Solstice
Sun, and what I see is
endless rays of blessings,

a halo of blessings raining
down upon Earth, us
humans (the real shock,
   the real awe)—I fill

my eyes with wonder, I am
hungry for wonder (while
   suffering giant flea bites
all over my body, saturated in

   anti-itch ointment, meds haha)—
Then, I hear it, the drumming,

the circle of drumming, black
men, brown men, some white

men, a young Asian girl, all
drumming—I sit close by
hungry for drums, my body
remembers JOY, sheer joy,

the dance—a crazy and
wise dancer passes through
the circle, circles the
circle, "Do you feel the

Sun Gods? Do you feel the
Sun Gods? Do you feel the
symp-toms? Do you feel the
symp-toms?" Lifting his shirt

to the wind, exposing dark
flesh the Sun has loved, smiling
the smile of innocent Sun
Child, this man of 50 something—

beautiful black woman with
dreads rises to dance with
her son in her arms, two women,
three women, four women, I join

them, I dance to the drums, to the
circle, to loved children, to the
Sun Gods, to the symp-toms,
I face the sea, the endless

rays of blessings falling falling
falling on each one, but can
we feel the symp-toms . . .
as I rest the crazy and

wise dancer passes me, looks
directly into my eyes, smiling like
the Great Sun, "You love me, but
I love you more."

Solstice, Venice Beach,
Drum Circle, June 21, 2003

El Sepetio

"The soul is in the face,"
Mamacita used to say,
Yaqui grandmother who raised
me in San Francisco's barrio,

The Mission—she never, ever,
slapped me, hit me, to control
me, hyper-energy-demon, she'd
make the sign of a spanking with

her hand, I'd laugh—then, in a
low, prophetic voice (in Spanish,
     of course), "Ayyyy niña,
ayyyy niña, El Sepetio will come

for you when you least expect it,
he's a beautiful young man with
a beautiful smile, but if you
look closely he has not shoes,

not feet, but hooves, and when
he takes you, for the bad things
you do to me, then you will see
his true face, el alma . . ."

Only this would stop the
hyper-energy-demon, make
me find a quiet corner by
my window (my favorite, rainy

     days with tears of the sky,
as Mamacita called rain, if I had
     to be inside). I would sit very
quietly, gazing out the window, vigilant

for the beautiful young man with hooves,
wondering where he came from, probably

Mexico, Mamacita's country, why he'd
follow her here, to help her with, yes,

me. And then, I wondered if
El Sepetio ever took her with
him, showed her his face, his
soul—this kept me in line

for years, until now.
O Sepetio, beautiful man with
feet like hooves, show me
your face. Your soul.

in Guad we trust

Fiesta Days, stage in
the plaza, Pueblo Indians
dance for the buffalo, the
hunt, rain, their rattles soothe

me like rain, clouds gather, no
thunder, lightning yet—across the
way Indians line clay colored
walls, sell jewelry made by their

own hands, such beauty, if only
we could buy the magic. Guadalupe
gazes out at all, her painted
self, her crowned self, her

Goddess Self—families, tourists, lone women, men,
older women in groups, teenagers, sexy couples,
stray drunks, we all gather in front of the stage,
drumming, dancing, rattles, clouds gather,

in Guad we trust.
Next, the Elvis impersonator, exciting
music, he takes the stage, small man,
balding with sideburns, well worn

Elvis outfit, and a Mexican El Vez at
that—giggles, waves of soft laughter.
Music, Elvis music, he begins to
sing, IT'S ELVIS!!! El Elvis

hands out silky scarves to young girls,
the older women, red-faced they wait
their turn, men go up to shake his
hand, the drunk asks El Vez to sing one

for his mother, he does, folks clap
for the spirit of El Vez. In this

place, Santa Fe, Holy Faith, magic
is created by hand, the tough cholo

biker takes his daughter to receive a scarf,
smiling widely when she does, El Vez is a
Mexican who dances for rain, clouds gathering,
rattles, drums. In this place, we believe.

Santa Fe, September 6, 2003

Zozobra

Old Man Gloom is ready to
burn, perched high over our
heads, bluish eyes, yellow hair,
an Indian teen says, "Fire up

the white guy!" The white folks
shift uncomfortably, the brown
folks just smile. Me, I didn't
write out my karmic garbage, bring

my filed divorce papers (my 20-year
marriage), or a copy anyway, old family
photos of me in the diaper business, the
Little League business, the track team and

the Planned Parenthood business, not to
mention the college scholarship and fund
business, then the "Who's the perfect parent
I did my best, better than best, you walked

away with my heart" business—
no, I didn't bring the paperwork to
be burned to healing ashes.
Two husbands, various lovers,

four grown children, healthy and
whole, whether they know it
or not, well that takes time, at
least into your forties, after

that you might miss the boat.
I won't speak of my childhood,
I'm too damned old for that, besides
I genuinely love my life now, at 59—

I'm in the pack-my-suitcase-lock-the-apartment-
drive-to-the-airport-travel-wander-teach-read-

my-work-for-joy-pay-apartment-as-I-left-it-
my-sheets-are-soft-I-go-to-Bali-Hawaii-

Mexico-next-Paris-Venice-Spain-my-
days-and-nights-are-mine-peace-and-
drama-unfold-in-oceanic-cycles-and-
I'm-right-here business. So, maybe

what I gave Old Man Gloom was the
ghostly me, the one trying to be born,
my daring, curious, naturally joyous
twin, that one. Me.

I gave him the ghost (as he screeched and yowled),
I welcomed the twin (as he went up in fireworks, smoke),
my soul holding hands with my spirit. Me.
Fire up the white guy. Healing ash. All of us.

The burning of Zozobra, Old Man Gloom,
Santa Fe, September, 2003

emperor of the moon

> Bush is an emperor.
> —Spanish president

The Emperor has spent 100 billion
(and more) tax dollars on his spectacular
Shock and Awe Show in Baghdad,
14,000, and growing, civilians *accidentally*

killed, our own young soldiers
committing suicide, hunger in our
own country, the wealthiest nation in
the world cuts breakfast programs

for schoolchildren, for some the main
meal of the day, cuts school
funding, larger classes, fewer teachers,
those teachers paid less, the violence

of the young in our country with no
moral leaders except that of the
Emperor who speaks directly to God,
and this God tells him to put that

100 billion, and growing, dollars into more
war and death, forget the hungry
children without medical coverage, when
they grow up to be violent just

build them arks in the shape of
prisons—this God tells the
Emperor to go to the moon, more
billions for the moon, and put a

cross on it while you're at it,
the hungry, starving, dying and
maimed will lift their eyes to the
moon for centuries to come, when

all the wild places are finally tamed,
slaves learn to serve their masters,
the starving die without a whimper, you
will be the Emperor of the moon.

> *To Emperor Bush, January 2004, and to all the*
> *entitled ones who believe they should feast*
> *while others starve, that they should live*
> *while others suffer, because they say so.*

dear world,
dear earth,
dear Ixchel,
dear Quetzalcoatl,

What is Manifest Destiny?
Is it me sitting by the spring-filled
creek, my car parked in the
slot for this place, picnic

table, the ancient trees whispering,
yellow monarchs, their huge
wings loudly slicing air, my
eyes resting on flowing light—

a woman brings her dog to the creek,
smiles, stands behind me as though
to say, I claim this place, she's
parked behind me, her area the

other side, same creek, same ancient
trees whispering, same yellow monarchs,
same diamondback rattlers, she and
her friend take my picnic table; as I pass,

"Did we swipe your table?"
I want to say,
"You've been swiping my
table for 1,000 years,"

instead I say, "It's all yours."
And why is this ancient place
called Bandelier, after the
so-called explorer's name;

I want the Tewa name, the one the
Pueblo man sang in the Sky Kiva

last October—I'm sick of the conqueror's
name on my tongue, "Tyuonyi," I whisper.

*   *   *

I go to my son's graduation in
Denver, Colorado, he in his robe,
I remember him, the lightning streak that
made me weep and laugh, with love.

His lovely, part Cherokee partner, her
people glowing in her warm, brown eyes,
they welcome me before her words—the
mayor of Denver gives a speech,

a talk about his grandparents that
I enjoy until, "The pioneers got the
arrows, the settlers got the
land." Is this Manifest Destiny?

No Indian people here, their tables
swiped, long gone; in Santa Fe (where
    I now live) he might get a few
arrows for that cute remark.

And finally, two dark
streaking military jets fly
over, the crowd cheers, I shiver
with the dread of civilian populations.

Later, a free barbecue, a blues band,
soul of slavery, swiped lives, bodies, true
words, "I got my mojo workin' but it sure don't
work on you .   ." Ain't that the truth, I laugh.

Is this Manifest Destiny?

*   *   *

USA jets bomb a home, a wedding,
in Iraq, suspected safe house for
terrorists, someone's home, someone's
wedding—they fired shots of joy

into the air, shots of celebration
(their culture, their joy, their gathered
    families, as this country gives them
    freedom—is this Manifest Destiny?) . . .

the jets were being fired upon—
over 50 celebrating people killed,
15 of them children, blown to
bits, decapitated, is this Manifest

Destiny? Are they free now?
Are the billions spent on 'war is peace'
(pacification, liberation) boosting the
world market, all that oil more precious

than mere human blood (including our own
    young soldiers), are they free now, are they
at peace? A child's head separated from her body,
are we free now? Are we at peace?

Is this Manifest Destiny?

              *   *   *

Forgive us, Allah, for we have
sinned—human blood finally not
more precious than oil—the Christian, Jewish Gods,
Great Spirit, all the Buddhas, Spider Woman, Changing
Woman,

healing Mayan Goddess, Ixchel,
know this, there is no manifest destiny,

only human cruelty, humanly made evil—
forgive us, Allah, for we have

forgotten human kindness, decency,
as we drop bombs on unprotected
homes, families pointing guns skyward
in celebration. Forgive us, the

conquerors, who have come to set
you free, to save your souls,
your oil wells, to wipe out our own evil—
I am so sick of the conqueror's tongue.

Salaam   Salaam   Salaam   Salaam

*In October 2006, over 600,000
Iraqi civilians have been "freed,"
killed.*

ACT

act

I completed the act
in my dream, to
my surprise, I did
the impossible.

Now, the impossible is
my journey, my life,
in dreams, to act in
impossible ways.

Dream

dreamers

All the dreamers
dreaming
me home to Bali,
an island of dreamers.

October 4, 2001

for sale

Chill day in Santa Fe, he sits on an island
between flowing cars with a sign
POETRY FOR SALE, I zipped
by then tried return, couldn't

reach him, my heart went out to him,
I was impressed, I wanted to buy a
poem—then I went to Bali, flying
through the night following the

lovely curve of spinning Earth through
darkness toward the Sun, morning
First Dawn, *heat*. There, I saw beauty
that stunned me silent, I could only stare

and stare mutely. Joy. And the
dances, the dances hold Good
and Evil, the struggle between them,
as the world dances its dance to stamp

out Evil, the senseless deaths in
New York, D.C., Pennsylvania, now
innocent people in Afghanistan—in Bali
people stop to ask where I'm from,

some place their hands over their hearts,
some take my hand in theirs, all
look right into my eyes, I say
"USA"—"Very sad, very sad what

happened in your country." "I cried
when I heard " "All religions, same
God." "Madame not afraid to come to
Bali, that's good." On Lake Bratan,

shrine to the Goddess, Dewi Danu Bratan,
I left a USA quarter, prayed for the highest good

for all beings in the cosmos, some things
for myself. When I went to the "toilet" as

it's called there, paid a woman 500 rupiah
for its use, deep basin of water and small
bucket by its side, when I tried to
flush with bucket, nada, then she

came in with a huge bucket full of water,
her brief sound of disgust, WHOOSH,
she returned as I washed my hands with
a chip of soap, smiling and selling me red

jeweled strawberries, 3,000 rupiah, I buy—
you shit, you eat, you dance the Evil and
the Good, sell your poetry—and pray for
the innocent everywhere, in Bali.

October 2001, our planet Earth
(On Sept. 11, 2001, 35,600 children died
from conditions of starvation worldwide.
—from the Food and Agriculture Organization
of the United Nations.)

male beauty

Every man is beautiful in Bali, a flower
behind his ear, the way they play
music for the women to sing
and dance—
and the men dance as well, becoming
graceful, gorgeous—here

I don't feel the usual violence toward
me, thoughts of rape—sexual interest,
yes, admiration yes, I'm even told
I'm beautiful in a simple
trusting way—and the young man

on Lembongan Island, we talked late into
the night, the ocean danced below
us, the moon chased the stars—
a young man with wisdom, the old
soul in his eyes burning, he looked
right into me without shame, and I looked

back. I rose to go to bed, to my room—
he said he'd be sleeping outside in the
canopy bed, in the soft wind, and that
I was the only guest on this side.
I bolted my door against the ocean, moon,

stars and wind. I bolted
the door against myself,
not him, not him—
at 3 a.m. I walked down the steps,
felt the ocean tug—I saw him
in the morning dressed in his sarong,

a flower behind his ear,
his eyes dark pools of
truth and desire.

I know he heard
the bolt lock,
but he didn't hear me
burn.

Bali, October 2001

trust

My plane reservations to Bali were made in March of 2001, and my tickets were non-refundable; even as I made them I thought, "Are you crazy? October is a long way off," (but these were the cheapest tickets and they were going fast). I would land in Bali on my fifty-seventh birthday, a twenty-year dream, literally. So, I made plane and hotel reservations and put them away in my travel folder, knowing there's really little anyone can control beyond dreams and wishes. Some writing students would join me for the first few days, then I'd be on my own. I welcomed the idea of company in the beginning, but I also know myself. I like to be alone (all one) to process and experience things as they come. The writer-at-large-in-the-world after forty years of being the daily parent.

How was I to know (how would any of us know . . .) I'd be taking off right after the tragedy and national sorrow, fears of traveling in Indonesia, or any air travel for that matter (every student cancelled). Yet I'd had a strange feeling of foreboding all year about the end of August; in a conversation with a local Native healer, he felt the same way. A global event, a feeling of warning that we couldn't name. And so, after final talks with two of my grown sons: "You should go, Mom, cause you'll be a royal pain in the ass if you don't."

"We'll raise the ransom if you're kidnapped; just go."

"Really?" I ask, touched at such a thought. Laughter. "Maybe."

But what really did it for me was the car I saw in traffic in Santa Fe, where I live (and what brought me here, "holy faith." what only the soul can see): its huge blue bumper sticker with TRUST in clear white letters. It looked newly bought, stuck on, just for me. Plus, I'd had no warning dreams (I'm Yaqui Indian, raised with belief in dreaming, by my grandmother)—some dreams of losing my money, so I bought a waterproof money belt and a regular cloth one.

My flights from Albuquerque to San Francisco, my fellow passengers, had a new tone of muted fear, deep sorrow, myself included. I too had been glued to CNN for days and nights, tuning in at 3 a.m. to make sure the world was still out there, somehow safe. I'd seen the images of the planes full of people—

living children, women, men—crashing into the World Trade Center and the courageous ones running in to save them.

I lit candles and mourned with everyone else, my country (my world). And then the reality, no air travel. I took the flag that came on the back of my newspaper, the *New Mexican*, wrote in pen where the white stripes are: ONE PEOPLE, ONE PLANET, HEAL US ALL, and taped it to my window. And I thought of my plane tickets to Bali and sighed.

And here I was, a few weeks later, in San Francisco Airport's International wing at the Eva Air counter, and the young Asian man telling me, "Your flights were cancelled, 911 in your country." I find myself insisting, "I paid for these tickets, I've flown in from New Mexico, and all my hotels have been paid for . . ." He smiles, turning into a computer whiz (the same trait I admire in my twenty-year-old son), and fixes all my flights, eight planes in all round trip. Except for the one in Taipei, Taiwan, which I must deal with, he says, when I land there. The final four-hour flight that'll take me to Bali. TRUST.

I enter the Eva waiting room at the gate with about twenty minutes to spare until boarding, and it's filled with Asian travelers going home, visiting home. I'm one of three non-Asians, so there's a mass moment stare of curiosity (plus I'm a woman traveling alone). I smile and sit down. On the plane—a triple-wide jumbo jet—the truly gorgeous stewardesses stand to greet us once we're all seated, and at the end of a very long announcement (first in Chinese, then English), the female voice says, "We are here to serve you," and then they bow to us. The gesture moves me, and I begin to relax, breathe.

At the end of the flight they bow again as the passengers clap, and they truly do serve us. I'm amazed, never having experienced this on domestic flights; courtesy, yes, but not *this*. We're given hot towels immediately and during intervals, snacks, dinner with wine (refills on wine and coffee, tea), *Moulin Rouge* with glowing Chinese subtitles.

Before we land in Taipei (the Republic of China), we're told in Chinese, then English, in a very lovely female voice, "We are required by law to warn you that anyone caught smuggling firearms or drugs into Taiwan faces the punishment of death. Thank you." Oh boy, I think, what the hell am I doing . . . but I continue to the Eva Air counter and wrestle for my new flight schedule to and from Bali. A minimal but firm show of persistence and everything works out well. My overnight lay-over on the way back, a stay in the Transit Hotel, right in the terminal, will be covered by Eva. My original flight from Bali was cancelled, so I have to leave one day early, damn.

I'm beginning to feel like a warrior on her quest, every problem a challenge—Bali or bust. And I secretly wonder if fanatic Muslims are waiting for a muy loca Americana to walk out of the Denpasar Airport; my one ace in the hole: "I'm from Mexico . . ." in a flow of irate Spanish, ha and ha.

My last contact from Bali was from a young woman named Dewi ("goddess" in Balinese—her name comforted me); we'd been zipping emails in the last few days. She works for a travel agency there, and is a student at the university. Me: "Tell me the truth, is it safe, Dewi?" Dewi: "My beautiful island is safe; you will love everything, believe me; come to Bali." TRUST.

After a four-hour flight, Bali. The first thing I feel is luxurious but real heat, and my body begins to manufacture moisture I didn't know I had to spare. The driver Dewi sends to pick me up is exactly my youngest son's age, twenty, and his Balinese name in English (he tells me after I ask if there's a translation for the long, beautiful-sounding name), is Love. He smiles widely and laughs with unselfconscious joy. Sheer joy that makes me laugh. In the next few weeks, I will come to know this smile, this laugh, as Balinese, and they will repeatedly tell me as a seemingly insurmountable problem arises, *"No problem."* At first I'm truly irritated—like maybe it's no problem to you—but after a few days I begin to smile at the words "No problem."

The traffic we encounter on the way from Denpasar to Ubud horrifies me—two lanes turn into three, four, even five and six as motorcycles pass us on both sides (I repeat, both sides); and people just being missed, including those walking with baskets balanced on their heads, children beside them, on the sides of the crazy roads. But I can't help noticing the flood of color, the woman we just missed wearing a bright flower-filled sarong, her hips moving to some slow, timeless beat in the frenzied traffic all around her; and me, of course, trying not to scream. I notice, again to my horror, that most people on motorcycles, including whole families with children (even babies being held), don't wear helmets. But I also continue to note the clamoring beauty, and I'm truly astounded. No one yells because they're almost hit, no one flips "the bird." In short, no "road rage"—nothing personal, no problem.

"These people are truly fearless!" I exclaim to Love in our new air-conditioned van.

"Fearless, what's that?" he laughs.

"It means you're not afraid to die."

He turns to me, laughing loudly. "That's good, very good, fearless, yes." I can see that my reincarnation beliefs will be put to a true test, and I smile, then wince as traffic continues on in normal Balinese style.

In Ubud I stay in a place of spectacular beauty (the Pertiwi Bungalows), where each morning a man places freshly blossomed red hibiscus flowers behind the stone ears of guardian frogs, monkeys, elephants, and at Brahma's dancing feet— where women in rainbow sarongs carry large baskets full of offerings and bundles of burning incense sticks to every altar on the grounds, morning and night. Even one small offering at the edge of the upper pool, as I silently watch her bless the place (me in the pool becoming water, slightly cooler than the tropical air).

At night I go to the dances and watch the grace, beauty, passion of women, men, girls, and boys dance the dance of Good and Evil, as the world dances its own dance, the same one really. These beautiful dances of Good and Evil always bring the world into balance, every time; I pray they do. (And then later watch the dancers drive away on motorcycles, two or three sharing one, no helmets, TRUST.) I arrive during a Hindu celebration that takes place once every generation, beginning just after my birthday on October 6. The Grand Ceremony is held in the Pura Dalem Ubud Temple and other temples throughout Bali.

The tourist booklet for the Grand Ceremony eloquently states, "This multi-faceted ceremony is being carried out to realign the world, which is currently out of balance; causing earthquakes, volcanic eruptions, war and chaos . . . It is hoped that the rituals being carried out will redress the problems faced today, and restore the earth to the proper balance." And on the cover, with a photo of a temple altar and offerings, two fringed umbrellas to each side, it says, "TO HARMONIZE THE

TEMPLE AND ITS PRECINCTS, THE VILLAGE AS WELL AS THE UNIVERSE" . . . TRUST.

These ceremonies take place from October 6th to the 28th. Groups of young boys and men will roam the streets playing music for the golden, long-tailed, regal Lion Barong (four feet showing underneath as they dance, sometimes twisting until head and feet meet, onlookers laughing). The large group of boys and men play music, sing, and chant as the Lion Barong dances for each home and place of business, blessing them for a few rupiah. I will see many barong dances in the streets in the days to come and women carrying lush temple offerings on their heads (stacks of fruit, food, flowers, stunning in beauty) as they walk in a line of all women in that slow (fearless), graceful walk.

Later I walk up the rice field road (behind my hotel) braving wildish Balinese dogs to avoid Mr. Wonderful on Monkey Street Road (where the Lion Barongs dance down). This is the name he gives me as he generates charm, enormous energy, trying to set me up for a "spectacular and cheap tour on a motorcycle." I can just hear my grown kids: "Leave it to Mom to die on a motorcycle in Bali with some guy named Mr. Wonderful." I will greet farmers as they pause in their work to smile and nod, and some people approach me with hands over their hearts, some taking my hand into theirs, all meeting my eyes deeply. I begin to anticipate these meetings with total strangers with a kind of little kid's pleasure. Joy.

I will gaze at the glowing, green rice fields with rainbow flags in the wind, set out to discourage hungry birds, temples with their daily offerings, and I will wonder at it. The sheer beauty of every day.

I will arrive at the Pura Dalem Ubud Temple, and be told I must dress properly in a sarong, sash, and a white Third Eye headband (I know about this, my Yaqui grandmother also wore one at home, and to sleep, for vision and dreaming). They lend me all this and I donate 50,000 rupiah, five dollars. The Temple is immense and ancient, and the stone stairs lead me upward. I will walk past a full gamelan orchestra of men, with small white, sweet-scented flowers behind their ears, playing very loud, beautiful music that seems to hold every human paradox (love/hate, war/peace, life/death, good/evil); and I will enter a room truly beyond description. Multicolored umbrellas (red, black, white, yellow for each deity and spirit of the earth and sky), silky and fringed, covering sacred space, tapering banners with small silver mirrors at their tips reflecting the sun, tables full of offerings, ancient stone carvings on every side; full-breasted Goddess with immense, outstretched wings emerging from stone to the right, and sitting in the center of it all, a courtyard full of women dressed in a rainbow of sarongs and lacy, see-through blouses with dark under-blouses. Some of the women have Third Eye headbands as I do; some don't.

They all sit directly on the stone and earth floor as the men play the lovely, fully human music in the next courtyard, and a shadow puppet master enacts a story with his mysterious puppets directly to my right. Two teen boys play a smaller, sweet-sounding gamelan softly, right behind the shadow puppet master. Then the women begin to sing in one full, feminine voice. This voice seems to come directly from their wombs, the dark place of creation, and all possibilities. I want to weep with joy (this is where I've always wanted to be, I feel), but I don't as I sit by the arched stone doorway with a sacred being, mouth open, roaring, carved at the top; and the ancient symbol of the swastika over it, symbol of eternity. I'm afraid to disturb them with my presence. After a while, a woman turns and motions for me to join them so I do (surprised and grateful), and as they pray silently, lifting one flower between clasped hands to their foreheads, then another flower from their offering baskets, I wish I had some flowers. I'm given flowers. This will often be repeated in Bali. I'll think it, then someone "hears it" and responds.

I will see the sacred *Bagia,* an enormous mandala symbolizing the entire universe created for the Grand Ceremony. It contains everything, all symbols of our world, the universe. "All the objects, creatures, elements, and features of the universe are represented in this gigantic, mountainlike offering."* It stands tall, and it's so full of color, such a vital sense of life, that each symbol seems to dance in this "mountainlike offering," and I literally open my eyes wider trying to take it all in. (I will dream in Bali as I've not ever dreamt before, supported by a tiny island of dreamers, and I will write them down to not forget.)

I will raise my palms with the other women as the grandmother sprays holy water on us (the light spray refreshing in the heat), and I will feel that I've finally, after fifty-seven years, arrived in the Room of Women where men with flowers behind their ears play music as they sing from their feminine centers. Where the grandmother will boss the young men around as they build a fire in the center of the courtyard, while everyone smiles, and then she'll angrily break a piece of bamboo in two, and toss it in the fire. Later, when people ask if I have children (I think a question asked automatically of women), I'll say I'm also a grandmother, while thinking of the grandmother in the temple, and a writer. I can see being a grandmother carries weight, so I enjoy it, but "the writer" part is not totally understood, and I sometimes have to describe a book that I write all by myself. Then the wonderful Balinese smile. "A writer, that's very good, yes."

And, as a part of the Grand Ceremony, they will carry sacred objects from nearby Pura Desa Peliatan—the temple to worship Brahma, God as Creator (DESA)—to Pura Dalem Ubud, the temple to worship Siwa, God as Destroyer (DALEM). The sacred objects will be carried in a grand procession in the afternoon from Desa the Creator to Dalem the Destroyer. Here they will bury the Bagia, exquisite and truly mountainlike symbol of the universe, beneath the foundations of the temple: "The procession and planting of the Bagia represent the belief that everything belongs to the universe, and that ultimately everything returns to it."*

I will wonder how many men will be required to actually lift it and take it to the mountainlike hole dug under the foundation for the planting—I wonder. And I will know the Bagia belongs to us ALL—Muslim, Christian, Hindu, Jewish . . . On the second page of the booklet there's a beautifully drawn symbol within a large circle—a beauty beyond words, I feel—then below it the words "There is only One Ultimate God, with no equal."* I take it that this One God contains all opposites imaginable; it makes me feel at peace just to gaze at the black-and-white symbol.

I will sadly leave Ubud (if I'd known about the Grand Ceremony I would've planned differently, of course), and go to Sanur by the sea. I rent a lounge chair for 20,000 rupiah, two dollars, for the day from a spiky-blonde Balinese surfer dude and receive a world-class, hour-long massage from his sister for

220

four dollars (ten-dollar tip; she's so happy) as her four-year-old daughter wanders in and out in the small clothing shop she runs, massage table in the back, fan churning. I'm so happy.

I will jump on her motorcycle, her four-year-old daughter in front of her, all of us with no helmets—me in a sarong flapping in the breeze as young Balinese men yell, "Mama mia!" as we pass. We almost get hit by a gigantic, gleaming tourist bus at the corner, no problem. She doesn't blink an eye, only a brief out breath of impatience and relief. I quickly wonder if my mangled body would be given a Grand Cremation Ceremony here (as I would prefer), or shipped home as stray baggage—no problem, no problem, I silently chant (I truly must believe in reincarnation as I seem to be passing the ongoing tests). Trust.

I will laugh as we zip further along, turn a corner hardly stopping, cars coming left and right (2, 3, 4, 5 lanes), as we arrive at my hotel in Sanur, no problem, so I can pay her for the beautiful patchwork silk and velvet jacket I bought from her. We will all sit on my bed and talk (her daughter munching on cookies), and I will pay her more than we agreed on during the bargaining process. We all smile.

I will take a ferry for a day trip to Lembongan Island, my final day in Bali, and find I can't leave at the end of the day, so I pay an extra 150,000 rupiah, fifteen dollars, for a room that sits on a cliff facing the ocean—I repeat facing the ocean—with a canopy bed, sacred images on the walls, and a seashell wind chime made into a light fixture. I will keep muttering, "I didn't even bring a toothbrush," all the while tensing up at the reality of my plane taking off the next day at 4 p.m. sharp (no problem).

I will hop on another motorcycle with another young man (my son) Jules's age, early twenties, and we'll ride over extremely potholed "roads" with chickens and roosters flying out of the way. He will take me to an underground house built by one man (from his sixties to his mid-seventies) entirely by hand, dug and carved out of stone, every stone room lit by lanterns. The sharp smells of stone, earth, and, I swear, the sweat of his work, greets me in the darkness between lantern flames. Then, he will take me to Secret Beach and Dreaming Beach and let me sit in silence for a while as I just open my eyes a little wider to take in this beauty. He will finally join me on the sand, and we'll talk about dreams on Dreaming Beach, and he'll say, "I'm so sad to hear about your country, we pray for better times, yes, Bali prays for your country." Followed by the wonderful Balinese smile (I forget about my plane, no problem).

I will go with him and his cousin on a boat they built with large red wide-open eyes painted on the front as they take an ominous-looking spear gun to go turtle hunting. "Good food," they laugh as I'm hauled aboard, literally (the boat floating up to my waist by the reef). They will drop me off at a diving platform and I'll suddenly remember that I forgot my suit at the bungalows. "NO PROBLEM!" they yell back at me, laughing loudly (that young man's sheer sense of joyousness that I love), as they leave, one standing with the spear gun on the bow as the other steers. And, after my moment of panic, I realize they're right—no one's around. I slip into the ocean, float, swim, float into rainbow fish, neon fish, small fish, big, colorful fish that make me hold my breath, my mouth around the snorkel . . . breathe, breathe . . . blue and purple coral, clusters of green living tentacles waving, unending as I float and breathe in the Badung Strait of the Bali Sea. Trust.

Then I will stay up late (after eating a perfect dinner of grilled morning-caught fish, rice, home grown vegetables), talking to one of the hotel's owners (Villa Wayan), whose Balinese name translates to Source of the Sun. He's also a spiritual leader of his village, his great-grandfather still a revered priest even after death, and a law student in Denpasar (about 45 minutes by ferry). He surprises me with a toothbrush and toothpaste, a vodka collins I ordered with the vodka floating over the halfway point, tonic in a bottle, and a small plate arranged with slices of lime.

"Mama mia," I laugh.

"Is it too much?" he looks momentarily concerned.

"No problem." I laugh again and he joins me.

We talk late into the night of the world, his world (Bali, Lembongan Island), and mine, the USA. He's traveled to New Zealand, Australia, and Japan, and wants to visit America. "My people consider me the lucky one," he says somberly, feeling the responsibility of it (he looks seventy-two or so). "I'm studying law to help them; my country has very complicated laws." Then he laughs and looks his true twenty-seven years. We will

222

also talk about matters of the spirit over the burning candle between us, the constant roar of the ocean below; and I have to remind myself he's only twenty-seven, with a piece of his great-grandfather's wisdom manifest in him.

He has to rise at 5 a.m. for a temple ceremony and I have to rise at about the same time to catch the public ferry, so I excuse myself and go to my wonderful room. My final night in Bali. I open my shutters wide so I can hear the Bali Sea in my dreams. He will sleep in the outdoor canopy bed in a covered pavilion; I wonder what he'll dream.

I will see him in the morning wearing his sarong and Third Eye headband (last night he wore jeans and a shirt); and I will tell him, "You look beautiful in your sarong," and he'll smile as we meet eyes and touch hands goodbye. A boy of seventeen or so will take me on a motorcycle to the ferry, and chickens and roosters will fly out of the way, and we will miss every huge pothole. Always trust.

And I will wade into the questionable public ferry (the one coming over was definitely spiffier), and watch the swell of early morning waves approach us over and over. The Balinese passengers don't look thrilled at all. In fact, they look slightly seasick and terrified (the fearless ones; I begin to worry). But we all make it, although the ferry doesn't quite make it all the way to shore, so an immense, muscular Balinese man carries us to shore for 20,000 rupiah, two dollars. I give him 40,000 rupiah (I'm getting very good at conversion; I calculate now almost instantly). I wonder if I'm becoming the fearless traveler I used to be from ten to twelve, when I used to ride my bike to Golden Gate Park in San Francisco and climb buildings under construction to the very top at twilight to dangle my feet over the edge of ten stories and watch the sun set. I hope so.

I will catch my plane with time to spare (no problem); and I will return next time with my own temple sarong, sash, and Third Eye headband (to help me truly see and dream). Over and over, I realize that "the trick" is to stay in the dream, to trust.

I think of the women in Afghanistan under Taliban rule who are buried alive, shot for begging in the streets though their children are dying of starvation, killed for teaching girls to read and write; and the men who are publicly executed for any dissent. Perhaps the horror of September 11 will save them as the bombs fall (and innocent life is also sacrificed, as innocent life was sacrificed in the USA), and so many countries worldwide are now on a unified course to stop terrorism. I believe that this common course must be sustained in the coming years (the next 1,000 years), as we learn slowly and painfully that "terrorism" is a symptom of the Third World's devastating poverty, their daily starvation. "According to the United Nations Food and Agriculture Organization (FAO), approximately 35,600 children died from conditions of starvation on September 11, 2001" (*Utne Reader,* Nov-Dec 2001).

I wonder about the infinite trust of the starving, the invisible, that my prosperous, mostly well-fed country doesn't *see or hear.* The horror of September 11 has woken us up to the invisible in our world, the unspeakable symptom called "terrorism" that cannot be tolerated, but must wake us up to *the whole world* as we learn to balance global trading with global sharing . . . *35,600 children died from conditions of starvation on September 11, 2001. . . .*

And I think of the Bagia planted under the foundations of Pura Dalem Ubud Temple (DALEM, God as Destroyer), and I suddenly know we are only in the throes of global transformation, as the God of Destruction readies us for the God of Creation (DESA). Yet human choices must be made; may we choose well. ONE PLANET, ONE PEOPLE, HEAL US ALL.

About fifteen years ago, I dreamt myself as a very old woman in a city where technology had ceased to work, and I was trying to warn the future about devastation. I gave this dream to one of the characters in my novel *Naked Ladies,* on the very last pages: "The radios no longer work, not even the clocks, the children are dying, the birds do not sing."

On the last page of the Grand Ceremony booklet:
"I bow to Thee O Divine Gayatri,
O Savitri, O Three Syllabled Mazdai;
O Eternal, Immortal Divine Mother of Mothers,
Let all the World have Peace and Happiness."

*Quotes from the Grand Ceremony booklet,
October 2001
Please reread the poem "Soft Chaos," pp. 95–96.

night dance

Stars dance their ancient tunes
strung on light
strung on light,

I get dizzy watching such acrobatics
as everything melts away
to light;

and the night has always played
such music
and the void has always sung
its hunger:

the wide expanse
the wide expanse

and I have always prayed for
daybreak, for Earth splitting
to Sun;

fear, fear: listen:

love is the dance,
the spinning harp.

*Sebastopol, California, in the old willow tree
house by the creek, at night, on my beloved
farm, where I grew food, children, poetry.
July 1975*

wings (fear and fearlessness)

When the bird flies,
spreads her wings,
in the new sun's
light, she fears

her error, she loves
her perfection, always
equally—only then,
only then, does she

fly.

       *   *   *

Whenever I dreamt falling as
a child, my Yaqui grandmother
told me, "In that moment of
fear, spread your wings,

fly," Every morning I told her
my dreams, she told me hers—
and when I first flew, we
celebrated with café con leche,

fresh pan dulce, still
warm from the corner
store in the Mission
(she carried me on her body,

she carried me on her wings,
   and then she let
me go).
In that moment,

that very
moment, spread
your wings,
fly,

I tell
myself fifty
five years later,
fly.

*   *   *

I am the five-year-old
girl who can't speak English,
your language burns my tongue,
tongue of the conqueror, Mamacita's

people, the Yaqui (her language so soft,
   sunrise and sunset prayers)—yet
because she spoke Spanish, I called
it mine, my mother

tongue. I am the girl who
can't speak English, who will
become a writer in the greatest
conqueror's tongue the world has

known thus far. In
my 60th year, I am the
woman who speaks and writes
in English. Fear and fearlessness

my wings.

*   *   *

I dream in Yaqui,
I know in Spanish,
I reveal in English,
I fly without

words.

May 2004, Santa Fe

eagle dancer

Indian Market, Santa Fe,
early morning rain, still
damp, all the tribes
gather, clouds gather,

light gathers, thunder gathers—
in the plaza CLAN-destine
plays Native rock and roll—
an eagle dancer spreads his

wings, wide open, eyes closed,
sweating in the noon sun, he swoops,
he staggers—a 2-year-old Pueblo boy
dances with him, he *sees* the eagle

dancing   dancing   dancing   flying—
he reaches out to a young Indian
woman, she *sees* the eagle dancer,
joins him, turning, twirling, holding

him up, the 2-year-old boy
dances at their feet, gazing up
at eagles, gathering clouds—
not once do his protective sisters,

mother, fear he'll be harmed, letting
him dance with eagle dancer, young
eagle woman (his daughter, sister, lover,
    mother) until the cops come to take

him away, drunken Indian, they
didn't *see* the sacred Eagle Dancer
flying through his clouds, Eagle Woman
at his side. That night the streets in

Santa Fe were raging
rivers, lightning piercing sky,

over and over, how he danced
us, the world, new.

August 21, 2004, Santa Fe Plaza

*On December 21, 2012, the Solstice Sun will align with
the center, the womb, of the Milky Way, a celestial event
that takes place once every 26,000 years. This is also the
date on which the Great Cycle of the Mayan Long Count
Calendar ends (only to begin again). Mayan astronomers
foretold that this date will mark a time when human
intelligence, spirit, will begin a new and creative age, the
Unfolding . . . into the Mayan Sixth World, the Pueblo
Fifth World.*